NANCY

3-3-04

NANCY

A Portrait of My Years

with Nancy Reagan

MICHAEL K. DEAVER

HarperLargePrint
An Imprint of HarperCollins*Publishers*

All photographs, unless otherwise noted, are courtesy of the Ronald Reagan Library.

Excerpt from Ronald Reagan's letter to Nancy Reagan on pages 250–51 from *I Love You, Ronnie* © 2000 by Ronald Reagan Presidential Foundation. Used by permission of Nancy Reagan and Random House, Inc.
Lyrics of "Second Hand Rose" as performed by Nancy Reagan, reprinted on pages 105–6 with permission of Nancy Reagan and The Gridiron Club, Washington, D.C.

HarperCollins books may be purchased for educational, business, or sales promotional use. For information please write: Special Markets Department, HarperCollins Publishers Inc., 10 East 53rd Street, New York, NY 10022.

FIRST EDITION

Designed by Renato Stanisic

Printed on acid-free paper

Library of Congress Cataloging-in-Publication Data

Deaver, Michael K.
  Nancy : a portrait of my years with Nancy Reagan / Michael K. Deaver.
    p. cm.
  ISBN 0-06-008739-0 (alk. paper)
  1. Reagan, Nancy, 1923– 2. Presidents' spouses—United States—Biography.
  3. Deaver, Michael K. 4. Reagan, Nancy, 1923—Friends and associates.
  5. Reagan, Ronald—Friends and associates. I. Title.

E878.R43D43 2004
973.927'092—dc22
[B]
                                        2003044280

ISBN: 0-06-058978-7 (Large Print)

04 05 06 07 08 WBC/RRD 10 9 8 7 6 5 4 3 2 1

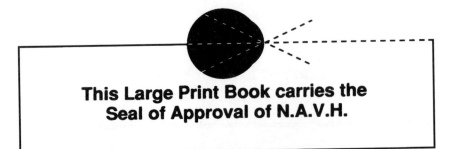

This Large Print Book carries the Seal of Approval of N.A.V.H.

To Bill Wilson and
Father Joseph Martin,
who gave me a new way of life

CONTENTS

NANCY

INTRODUCTION:

KNOWING NANCY DAVIS REAGAN

The phone in my den at home chirped quietly late on the morning of April 11, 2003. I knew who it was—the same friend who has called me at just about this time on the same date for the last three decades or so. In fact, I had been anticipating the call for most of the morning.

"Happy birthday!" Nancy Reagan said in a soft, pleasant voice before I could even get in a hello. As usual, she was the first person outside my immediate family to take note of the day.

"So, how old are you again?" she asked with a laugh, knowing the answer full well.

When I confirmed that, yes, I was sixty-five, she pretended to be taken aback.

"You can't be!" she said.

"What you're really saying is you couldn't be over eighty!" I said.

And so it went—variations on a continuing conversation that carried us back through a

White House and a statehouse, to a time before I was married and Nancy was just learning what it means to be a politician's wife. We ended our birthday talk that day as we usually did, with a keen grasp of the obvious: neither of us was getting any younger. But after I thanked her for the call and tried to settle back to whatever I had been doing, I found myself reminiscing about these ritual birthday wishes and how they came to be. Most of all, though, I was thinking of Nancy Reagan.

Ever since the mid-1960s, we had been the most unlikely of friends. I hadn't been a Reagan man early on, but I lived and breathed electoral politics. Even back then, when Ronald Reagan was just beginning his meteoric rise to the presidency, Nancy tolerated politics only because she knew her husband was called to serve. In truth, I had been frightened to death the first time Nancy and I talked, although I tried not to show it. I can't imagine she was overly impressed by the untested aide who had been assigned to her, either. But we got past all that, just as we would get past the inevitable peaks and valleys of our thirty-five-plus years of friendship.

We had shared Ronald Reagan's two terms as governor and three full-scale presidential campaigns. I had been by the Reagans' side when they moved into the White House, and I had been there again when he claimed his second four years in historic fashion. Nancy and I had traveled the globe together, and we'd spent more hours than either of us cares to remember plotting the minutiae of her husband's daily coming and going. I had stood next to the president as a bullet nearly pierced his heart, and I had been the first person to tell Nancy that Reagan had been hit. She and I shared the pain of that moment and many others, including the pain of the horrible disease that struck Ronald Reagan just as they were finally settling into a long-deserved retirement.

The more I thought about Nancy and mused on the journey she has made—from a single mother's daughter to Hollywood, the White House, and the unwinnable battle against Alzheimer's she now wages—the more I realized that Nancy's life has the arc of great drama.

Or maybe I should say "lives," because there have always been two Nancy Reagans: the one the public thought it knew and the private one that was revealed to just a few of us. The Nancy with whom most Americans are familiar had closets crammed with fancy clothes and a Rolodex full of rich and powerful friends. If you crossed her, you paid for it. If you tried to cross her husband, you paid worse. Nancy might have sat and stared in rapt admiration whenever Reagan got in front of a microphone, but those claws were sharp. You didn't want to take your eye off her for a moment.

The press loved to point out how Nancy hob-nobbed with celebrities from Frank Sinatra to Truman Capote, but the scribes seemed never to notice that she was also devoting hours upon hours to people who will never have their fifteen seconds on "Entertainment Tonight." Style columnists would write about Nancy and Betsy, Nancy and the White House china, Nancy and this-and-that, but there were precious few column inches devoted to Nancy and the Texas mother who called her because she had no other hope for her drug-addicted son, or Nancy and the wounded Vietnam vets she spent hours sitting quietly with, holding their hands.

The private Nancy, the one I've come to know over thirty-five years, is far more complicated than the stereotype. Nancy is no cardboard cutout. She's pure flesh and blood, with all the human strengths and frailties that entails.

In the Reagans' fifty-plus-year marriage, Ronald Reagan always received top billing, and Nancy wouldn't have it any other way. Like me, she is convinced that her husband was one of the great men of the twentieth century—a rare world leader who changed the tide of history. You don't upstage such a man, even if you want to, and Nancy has always wanted to do just the opposite. But I know, perhaps as well as anyone can, that Nancy has been no bit player in the story. Ronald Reagan would not have risen to such distinction without Nancy at his side. Of this, I am certain.

To a man incapable of protecting himself from those who served him poorly and even wished him harm, Nancy brought discipline. I don't want to even think of the problems Ronald Reagan would have encountered in both Sacramento and Washington if Nancy hadn't been quietly guarding his flank all those years. You would do just as well to come between a bear and its cub as try to come between Nancy and Reagan.

To a man who always had trouble expressing intimacy, Nancy gave the gift of her unrestricted love. She was his respite, his comfort, his reward at the end of the day. Whenever she left him to travel, the leader of the free world was anxious as a schoolboy until she was safely home again.

Now to a man no longer capable of looking after himself, Nancy is everything there is left to be: caretaker, guardian, nurturer of the Reagan legacy. Medical science doesn't give us much hope that Ronald Reagan even knows who Nancy is anymore, but Nancy, I feel certain, has no doubt on that score: their bond has always been too great to be broken by Alzheimer's.

Not long ago, I told about my life with Ronald Reagan in my book **A Different Drummer**. I now realize that you can't tell his story without telling hers. What follows are my best recollections and remembrances of those thirty-five years working with Nancy Reagan to protect, support, and help her "Ronnie" achieve his goals. It is, above all else, the story of a remarkable woman.

1

THE EARLY YEARS

Like so much else of my own history, the story of how I first came to know Nancy Reagan begins with her husband. In November 1966, Ronald Reagan delivered a body blow to the national political establishment when he was elected governor of California. His opponent, two-term Democratic incumbent Pat Brown, dismissed Reagan as a fading matinee idol turned political novice. East Coast liberals ridiculed him as a knee-jerk Goldwaterite and corporate pitchman. To a greater or lesser degree, Reagan was all those things, but his detractors missed the critical element: Ronald Reagan talked to voters in an idiom they could understand about issues that resonated deeply across the political spectrum. When the dust settled, the ex-actor had trounced the consummate politician, showing Pat Brown the door by a million votes.

The 1966 elections were good to me, too. I

had been overseeing three state assembly races in coastal California for Republican candidates and had managed to bring home two winners, thanks in part to Reagan's surprising coattails. But I hadn't climbed on the new governor's bandwagon early on when it counted, and even after the campaign was over, I still didn't know much about Ronald Reagan and even less about California's new first lady, Nancy.

Unlike most GOP field men who had been working the state that year, I also had little interest in joining the governor-elect's team in the capital city. I was living in Santa Barbara, with its Mediterranean climate, inviting beaches, and tile-roofed homes. I couldn't imagine giving that up for Sacramento, a sweltering valley town like Bakersfield, California, where I was born. For my money, Santa Barbara was heaven on earth. Sacramento was close to its opposite.

I also liked my work. I had become fixated with the power of advertising and creative direct mail in political races, and I had been able to field-test both—to great success—in the campaigns I had just managed. My immediate strategy was to join a small advertising firm in Santa Barbara, where I could continue to refine my techniques. From there, I liked to imagine a career path that ascended to the top of the ad industry.

A few weeks later, I took a call from Reagan's new handpicked chairman of the state Republican Party, Denny Carpenter, and put my plans for becoming Mr. Madison Avenue on temporary hold. Denny told me I was needed up north. Specifically, I was to report ASAP to William P. Clark, one of the chiefs of Reagan's transition team. I don't know why I got the call—presumably my old friend and political guru Stu Spencer had put them on to me. But there I was, Bill Clark's number two man overnight.

The transition team gave me a fascinating look inside state government. I was meeting great people and adding muscle to an otherwise fairly puny résumé. But I was also a short-timer. Chances were, I would retreat back to Santa Barbara without ever meeting California's new first couple, much less saying an intelligible word to either one of them. And that's almost the way things worked out.

On January 3, 1967, I watched as Ronald Reagan raised his right hand and took the oath of office. Nancy, of course, was at his side. The hour was late. Irked by the unseemly blitz of judicial and commission appointments that Pat Brown was doling out to his friends, Reagan asked to be sworn in at the "earliest possible moment." That earliest possible moment came at 12:14 A.M. Despite the hour, many of the Reagan campaign people were jubilant, to the point of welling up. They were finally seeing the fruits of a most difficult, unexpected journey.

I would see that same jubilation again in 1980, in Washington, not Sacramento, and from a much better seat. This time, though, I was in the peanut gallery—a transition staffer with neither the history nor the political juice to command a choice vantage point. Still, even watching from a distance, I found myself wondering if I would ever be involved in a cause so great that it would make me as emotional as those young staffers.

The next morning, still thinking about commitment, the Reagans, and Santa Barbara, I walked into my office ready to say good-bye. The transition was done; it was time to start governing. An hour or so later, Bill Clark asked if I would stick around and be his assistant in the cabinet affairs office. With little thought, I found myself saying yes. Sunny Santa Barbara suddenly seemed very far away.

I accepted the offer so quickly in part because I was warming up to Sacramento. As a conservative, I was both enthusiastic about Ronald Reagan's programs—although I still had trouble believing he was actually the governor—and curious about his capacity to lead. Reagan's promise to be a "citizen-governor" held real appeal to me, as it obviously did to millions of other Californians, but I wondered to myself just how effective a man with no elective experience could be in handling one of the nation's toughest political jobs. In truth, too, I had enjoyed my small

introduction to political power during the transition. Managing campaigns was exhausting but
exhilarating. Who knows, governing might be
fun, too.

Reagan had been in office about six months
when his chief of staff and deputy chief quit
abruptly, and the governor appointed my boss,
Bill Clark, to the top post, and Bill made me his
deputy. Until then, I had flown almost entirely
under the radar, one of many relatively inconse-
quential staffers. Now, amazingly, thanks to the
staff shake-up, I was a "senior administration official": the figurative, if not the actual, number
two man in the statehouse, complete with a well-
appointed office directly across from the governor of California.

Mind you, I had spoken no more than five
words to Ronald Reagan since first seeing him a
year or so earlier in Los Angeles at the Ambassador Hotel. He still had no idea who I was even
though I would be moving just a few doors down
from him. I'd said even fewer words to his wife,
but Bill told me I'd be her contact within the inner circle. Contact? I remember thinking. Why
would the first lady need any contact in her husband's office? If she had anything to ask the governor, why didn't she just bring it up with him
over dinner? I still had much to learn about politics, and the Reagans.

Bill Clark had handed his green, twenty-nine-year-old sidekick a pretty impressive roster of duties. Always interested in policy, Bill dove zealously into the budget, appointments, and all the serious stuff of high office. My official job description called for me to oversee the governor's schedule, serve as political liaison to other governors and politicos, and spearhead special events. In my eyes, these were plum assignments. The Nancy Clause was the only disconcerting part of the package.

From inside the governor's office and elsewhere, the reviews on Nancy Reagan were not good. Campaign staffers told me "Mrs. Reagan," as she was always referred to, had been difficult to handle. Others described her as impossible to placate, a tough-minded political wife who needed constant attention. "Demanding," "impatient," and "cold"—these words came up a lot in the halls when the subject turned to the first lady. "Dragon Lady" did, too. And a few other words best not repeated. Nor was the staff nickname for my new assignment, "the Mommy watch," particularly encouraging. It all sounded pretty scary to me, especially since I had almost zero knowledge of my new charge. I decided I had better do some homework, posthaste.

Like everyone else in California, I knew that she had been an actress, but for the life of me, I couldn't remember a single movie that Nancy Davis, as she was known in her professional days, had appeared in. There was also "The Stare," the un-wavering gaze she fixed on her husband whenever the two of them appeared together in public. (More on the famous stare later.) It wasn't much to go on, but it was all I had. Happily, as things turned out, I was about to get a graduate-level tutorial in the first lady, taught mostly by the subject herself, and it would begin on the first day of my new job as the governor's deputy chief of staff.

When my secretary announced, "Mrs. Reagan is on the line," I didn't know whether to jump out of my skin or hide under the desk. I was terrified. What if she asked me something I didn't know anything about? What if she was as formidable as everyone said she was? I would have liked some time to compose my thoughts, but here the governor's wife was, holding on the phone. I didn't have much choice but to pick it up.

"Hello," I said with feigned confidence.

She politely introduced herself as "Nancy Reagan" and quickly got down to business, speaking to me as if I had been doing this job for years. She was calling, she said, because she needed to change the governor's schedule so he could attend an event she was planning in Los Angeles for later in the week. She wanted "Ronnie"—the first time I had heard him called that—to make the trip for reasons she didn't share with me. I picked up the schedule and gave it a quick look.

Clearly, her planned trip to L.A. would conflict with important state business in the capital. Somehow, I managed to tell her with great calm that the assembly would be meeting that day and it would send the wrong signal for the governor to be out of town so early in the session. If she really needed him to be with her, I suggested, maybe she should consider rescheduling her trip when the assembly was out of session.

There was a terrifying silence on the other end of the phone, just long enough to imagine myself being chased back to Santa Barbara with my tail between my legs. Finally, she said something like, "Oh, dear, I'm sure you're right." She asked about some other dates, said good-bye, and hung up.

That was it. Flames hadn't shot out of the handset. State marshals didn't bust down my door as soon as we were through and order me to start packing.

"Whew," I thought to myself. "Just maybe this job is doable."

I was congratulating myself for my brilliance in conflict resolution when it occurred to me that what I had done was simply give the first lady the facts. I didn't try to finesse her. I hadn't talked too much. I wasn't out to impress her. (I was far too scared to attempt that.) I hadn't talked down or up to her or tried to bullshit my way around her. I'd just been myself.

Maybe the secret in dealing with Nancy Reagan wasn't to tiptoe past her or try to steamroll over her—impossible in any event. Maybe, I realized, the secret was to employ a radical, groundbreaking tactic: treat her like a human being. Most important, tell the truth. This has been the foundation of our relationship from that day to this one. Instead of viewing Nancy as the "Mommy" I would have to watch over, and watch out for, I began to see her as a valuable member of the staff, someone who would have many good ideas and a few clunkers but who would always be thinking about the endgame. After all, we shared the same interests: helping a guy named Reagan do the best he could as governor and look good while he was at it. If he was going to govern, she wasn't going to let him fail.

I once wrote that if Ronald Reagan had owned a shoe store, Nancy would have been out there pushing the oxfords and flat-heel pumps and ringing up sales on the register. She would have been happy doing it, too, and just as intent on making certain her husband succeeded in the shoe trade as she was on seeing him succeed in the political one. It was always about him.

Somebody was watching over Ronald Reagan by giving him Nancy. And Reagan knew this long before me or anyone else. He once said, "Nancy came along and saved my soul." She may have saved his political career as well, and when you consider who she was and where she came from—the **real** Nancy, not the cutout one—that's pretty amazing.

Born Anne Frances Robbins after her two grandparents, she was always called Nancy. As I was writing this book, I asked her why. I'd never known how she got the nickname, and I had never thought to ask her before. She told me she had no idea. If I was really interested, she said, I should ask her first cousin Charlotte. But neither Charlotte nor Nancy's brother, Dick Davis, knew the origin of the nickname.

The year of her birth remains an even greater mystery. When Nancy was just starting out onstage, she adamantly refused to answer a reporter's query about when she was born. Later when the story was published, Nancy was chagrined to note that the scorned scribe had made her five years more senior than she really was. She promptly wrote to the editor asking where she could get her five years back as she had "big plans for them." All of that, though, still begs the question of what year she was actually born. You couldn't get that from her at the point of a gun.

When she was still young, her mother, Edie, formally Edith Luckett Davis, used to tell Nancy, "A woman who will tell her age will tell **anything**." That's all her daughter needed to hear.

Nancy's birthday is no problem: she was born on July 6. But depending on whom you talk to, the year was either 1923 or 1921. Several years ago, we jokingly decided that Nancy should be ten years Ronald Reagan's junior. That makes 1921 official . . . but don't try to hold her to it.

Nancy's biological father, Kenneth Robbins, was a no-show at her birth. A journeyman who dabbled in many different career directions, from shoe sales to booking actors, he never quite settled on one he liked. She would see him during her life, but they had no real relationship to speak of. Edie and Robbins were married in 1917, and he ducked out when Edie was three months pregnant. Five years older than her short-lived husband, Edie would have to go it alone. Fortunately, she **did** have a career to fall back on; in fact, she had had one for a long time.

Edie began acting in 1900 at the age of three, bringing down the house without saying a word in the role of a dying child. Playing with stock companies along the Atlantic seaboard, she appeared onstage with some of the great ones: Spencer Tracy, George M. Cohan, and Walter Huston. Her favorite was Alla Nazimova, the Russian-born silent film star who had studied acting under the great Stanislavsky and who once commanded a higher salary per film than Mary Pickford. Alla was Nancy's godmother.

In time, many of Edie's pals would desert the

East Coast stages for the glamour of Hollywood. Edie, though, worked hard to keep her theater career alive even after her husband disappeared. After Nancy's birth, Edie became one of the earliest practitioners of "take your daughter to work day." With barely enough money to eat and keep a roof over their heads, Edie didn't have the luxury of a babysitter, much less a nanny. Much of Nancy's first two years were spent backstage while her mother rehearsed and performed. Nancy would show up literally everywhere with her mom, whether it was a society party in the Hamptons or a post-curtain-call reception.

As Nancy was nearing two years old, Edie decided a more stable environment was in order and asked her sister, Virginia Galbraith, to keep Nancy. The Galbraiths lived in the Washington suburb of Bethesda, not far from where my wife, Carolyn, and I live today. It was a quintessential middle-class existence. Virginia's husband, Audley, was a clerk at the railroad. Their daughter, Charlotte, was a few years older than Nancy. Over the half dozen years the two girls shared the same home, Nancy and Charlotte became like sisters.

It speaks volumes of Nancy that she turned out so well after being separated from her mother for six years. I'm sure it hurt, but she told me she came to believe the separation made her appreciate Edie so much more than she might have otherwise. That was certainly the case whenever I saw the two of them together: They seemed to have a special affection for each other. And it wasn't as if they never saw each other while Nancy was living with the Galbraiths. She and her aunt would visit Edie whenever she was performing in the Big Apple. Once again, Nancy would find herself backstage, soaking up the sight, sounds, and smells. Now, though, she was old enough to remember the experience and to want to take her own turn in front of the footlights.

In 1929, one of Edie's surprise visits to Bethesda would change Nancy's life forever. Nancy remembers her mother asking her to come outside. She knew immediately that something big was happening, but she couldn't know how big. Her mother had come to tell Nancy about the new man in her life, Loyal Davis. She had met Davis on board a transatlantic cruise headed to England. She was headed to an acting job; he was on his way to a medical convention. It was one of those moments when everything was right for romance. The two of them were to be married, and that meant Nancy and Edie could be reunited. Davis was a highly respected Chicago neurosurgeon. They would be moving in with him, on tony Lake Shore Drive. After half a dozen years of living off the kindness of relatives, Nancy suddenly found herself on the debutante track.

Everything Nancy has told me about Loyal Davis leads me to believe he was an old-school father. A disciplinarian, he believed in formality, work, and traditional values. Nancy actually called him Dr. Loyal for years. As for the good doctor, he had decided to never force himself on his stepdaughter. She could warm up to him at her own pace. In fact, the plan could not have worked better. Nancy came to love Loyal Davis and accept him completely as her father, and he wound up adoring Nancy as much as he did her mother.

By the time I came into Nancy's life, everybody just assumed that Loyal Davis was Nancy's father. I remember being on a campaign plane in 1968 when the first lady's press secretary, Nancy Reynolds, received a request from an earnest young writer for **Look** magazine. She wanted to know the name of Nancy Reagan's "real" father. Confused, Nancy Reynolds dutifully approached her boss and relayed the request. California's first lady responded immediately, if not defensively, "Loyal Davis."

That's what I thought, Nancy Reynolds said to herself as she reported back to the **Look** writer.

"Her father's name is Loyal Davis."

"I know who her **adoptive** father is," the reporter countered. "What I want to know is who is her **real** father."

Even more confused, Reynolds went back to Nancy Reagan a second time. The response was just as prompt, but slightly icier.

"My father is LOYAL DAVIS."

The next words from the reporter stunned Nancy Reynolds: "I know for a fact that Nancy Reagan is adopted, and I want to know who is the father."

Caught between two determined women and with no idea what the actual answer was, Nancy Reynolds tried one more time.

"Mrs. Reagan, I'm sorry, but **Look** says you're adopted, and they want to know the name of your real father."

"My father's name is Loyal Davis. End of story."

This could have gone on for hours if the flight had been New York to L.A. Thankfully, it wasn't. The pilot asked passengers to take their seats just about then, and Nancy Reynolds was spared any further humiliation.

That plane trip with the **Look** reporter was the first time I fully realized the deep loyalty to family and friends that runs through Nancy's being; it was fierce then and remains so today, in sickness and in health, in bad times as well as good ones. Nancy was at Loyal Davis's side when he died in 1982; she sat and held his hand for an hour after he was gone.

Look ran its story after that encounter on the

plane, including Nancy's insistence that Loyal Davis was her father. I can recall her worrying after she read it that her biological father might take offense, but she didn't have the least regret about the answer she had given, and in fact, she hadn't told even a white lie. In the late 1930s, still a teenager, Nancy had hunted down Kenneth Robbins and had him sign away his paternity rights. This story tells you a little about what type of woman Nancy was becoming. Just about to leave Chicago for a Bermuda holiday with friends, she approached her stepfather and explained that she wanted to stop in New York to meet with her biological father. When Loyal asked why, she explained that she wanted to ask Kenneth Robbins in person if he would sign the papers required to let Loyal Davis become her real father.

"I thought it was my job to do it," she told me. "I wanted to ask him myself."

In New York, Nancy met Robbins and his mother—Nancy's grandmother—at the Biltmore Hotel to go over the papers. Nancy recalls Robbins's being courteous and accommodating. He showed no sign of sadness or anger. His mother, on the other hand, seemed morose. "I could tell my grandmother was hurt," she told me recently.

Nancy did keep in touch with Mrs. Robbins. In fact, just after she and Ronald Reagan were married in the early fifties, Nancy got a call from her saying that she was going to be in Los Angeles and would love to see the newlyweds. The Reagans took her to their favorite haunt, Chasens. Without warning, while the three of them were waiting for a table, the elder Mrs. Robbins had a minor stroke. Alarmed and not quite sure what to do, Nancy called her adoptive father, Dr. Davis, for advice. Davis agreed it merited medical attention and dispatched a nearby physician friend to tend to her. Coincidentally, on the way out of the restaurant, with Mrs. Robbins on a gurney, the Reagans ran into Ron's first wife, Jane Wyman, and all of Nancy's segmented life seemed to come together, she said, if only for a few minutes. Fortunately, Mrs. Robbins would recover from the stroke.

Nancy was to grow up idolizing a set of parents who could not have been more different—not unlike herself and the man she would eventually marry. Her father was a take-no-prisoners, law-and-order man; her mother, a carefree Bohemian actress, as loose a goose as ever lived, it sometimes seemed.

In my view, Nancy was much more influenced by Loyal Davis than by Edie. He brought discipline to her life, a dignified grit that was totally at odds with the freewheeling Edie. I would see it every day—even now—in the form of her punctuality, directness, and drive. In terms of personality, Nancy is clearly her father's daughter.

I can personally attest to Edie's, shall we say, unconventionality. Once back in my early Sacramento days, a new secretary was earnestly trying to screen my callers. Apparently, she was having trouble getting any information out of one person who insisted she needed to talk with me about an upcoming event. Frustrated by the receptionist's multiple requests for information, the caller finally shouted, "Look, I don't want to date him; I just want to talk to him."

Edie was patched right through. She was then nearing seventy years old.

Tiny and sparkling, Nancy's mother seemed to know everybody, and she was loved and respected by them all. From LBJ to Billy Graham, Chicago mayor Richard Daley, and J. Edgar Hoover, they all took her calls. Daley, in fact, was an old friend. She chatted everyone up: beat cops, baseball players, ward heelers. Just to keep in practice, Edie would hit on Reagan's security guys all the time. They loved it. And nobody—least of all, Ronald Reagan—could resist her countless naughty stories. Edie and Reagan traded jokes regularly. Indeed, the only person Edie didn't share jokes with was her daughter.

"Nancy never 'gets' a good story," Edie

lamented to me one day. "Why the heck waste one on her?"

I feel the same way about the one and only movie recommendation I ever made to the Reagans. The film was **Kiss of the Spider Woman,** starring William Hurt and Raul Julia. Hurt won an Oscar for best actor, playing a homosexual locked up in a South American jail with a revolutionary played by Raul Julia. A gay and a radical in the same cell—it wasn't a sex picture, but it was a little on the edge. I urged Nancy to watch it during a long weekend at Camp David. Sure enough, she and Reagan did. The next week, she couldn't wait to get her hooks into me.

"Mike, how could you recommend that film?" she protested. "It was dreadful. We turned it off halfway through the reel."

I tried to make my case. "Once you get past the subject," I protested, "it was an incredible picture."

"Yes, but how do you get past that?" she asked.

I should have known better. Nancy was no prude, but both the Reagans were concerned about the coarsening content in movies in the 1980s. Reagan was always put off by foul language, and he resented the way actors cussed just to get a rating. He used to point out that he acted in the days when "you could do an entire love scene with your clothes on."

"I have always thought it was more suggestive," he once told me, "to see a hand reach out and hang a 'Do Not Disturb' sign on the door."

Nancy left home for Smith College, majoring in drama and graduating with the class of 1943 (which makes that 1921 birth date sound more and more accurate). Back in Chicago, she worked at Marshall Field's flagship department store for a while, but like her mother, she eventually migrated to the bright lights of Broadway. Unlike her mother, though, Nancy had an impressive pack of guardian angels waiting in New York and later in Hollywood. Clark Gable, Walter Huston, Mike Wallace, and others all helped keep an eye on their beloved Edie's daughter.

Then as now and probably as forever, contacts count in the movie industry. Nancy obviously had good ones, and she earned good reviews on her own, especially playing opposite Ray Milland in the highly regarded **Night into Morning.** In the normal course of events, she would have had a long, distinguished career in film. Instead, she was caught up in the scourge of the late 1940s: the hunt for Communists. It's laughable now: the wife of the president who did more than anyone else to tear down the Iron Curtain branded as a fellow traveler. But there Nancy was in a key movie trade publication, identified as a red sympathizer. Clearly, someone had made a mistake— Nancy was apolitical at the time—but if she couldn't rectify the situation, those years of hard career building in Hollywood might go down the drain.

Nancy asked her studio contacts what she should do. One piece of advice she received was to get in front of the president of the Screen Actors Guild, a guy named Reagan. Nancy knew of Reagan, naturally, and she jokingly figured that she could kill two birds with one stone: clear her good name and get a date with one of Hollywood's most eligible bachelors. A mutual friend, the prolific director Mervyn LeRoy, arranged for Reagan to call Nancy to discuss the situation. Nancy sat by the phone that evening, to no avail. Mervyn bumped into Nancy a few days later and reported that bachelor Reagan had called **him** back, not Nancy, to report that his research indicated there were a handful of other Nancy Davises out there.

"That's the problem," Reagan advised. He went on to say that the Guild would be happy to defend this particular Nancy Davis if formal charges of being a Commie ever got legs in Washington or anywhere else. For constituent services, Reagan was receiving high marks, but "One Take"—as Reagan was known, for his ability to get a scene right the first time—was obviously missing a few cues on this one. Disappointed but not ready to give up, Nancy told LeRoy, "I'd feel a lot better if Mr. Reagan explained it to me himself."

This time, Reagan did come to the distressed damsel's side, calling Nancy a few hours later with an offer to discuss her problem over a hot meal that evening. "It can't be a late night," he cautioned, "because I have an early call in the morning."

Nancy agreed to the impromptu dinner, but she couldn't hide her smile. "Early call" was an actor's dating insurance program in those days in Hollywood. If the evening was going well, he could just forget the next morning. If not, early call was the preferred excuse for the old "dine and ditch." The Gipper was going to show up. How late he stayed was the question.

Nancy recalls the first close-up of her future husband with great clarity. "Ronnie always looked even better in person than on the big screen," she remembers. On this evening, though, the "Errol Flynn of the Grade B's," as he had become known, came with a cane. Reagan had injured his leg in a basketball game.

Still clueless as to Nancy's larger intentions, Reagan got straight to work as soon as they met, brainstorming on Nancy's "Communist problem." By the time they took their seats at the restaurant, he thought he had the answer. "Have the studio change your name. You would hardly be the first."

That went over like a lead balloon—having waited so long to have a father, Nancy wasn't going to rush into giving up his name—but Reagan was scoring well all the same. He was anything but standard-issue Hollywood, Nancy realized. He lived in a world bigger than movies, and unlike many actors, he was able to see beyond himself. Reagan actually asked questions about her as the evening progressed. More amazingly, his curiosity seemed genuine. Once they had laid the Communist problem to rest, Reagan talked about his ranch and horses, American history, the Guild, and the wine—all big plus marks to Nancy's well-tuned ears.

Reagan, remember, wasn't the only eligible person at the table that evening. Nancy was fielding as many date requests as he was. She was nearing thirty by then (or perhaps already there) and hadn't had a really serious beau since a Princeton boyfriend was killed by a New York–bound train just as the United States was entering World War II. Since then Nancy had spent nights out with some of Hollywood's leading men but always seemed to find something missing before the evening was out. This night was shaping up differently.

In fact, by the end of dinner Reagan forgot about his "early call" and suggested a few drinks at a club where Sophie Tucker was singing. Nancy agreed but "just for the first show." They were still at the club when Sophie, "the Last of the Red-Hot Mamas," came out for her third set.

After that night, things just fell naturally into place. As the new couple dined together over the next several days, hitting the hottest spots in town, the trade press began making sounds about love at first sight and marriage. But the flashbulbs and flying champagne corks weren't their style. Soon, they would show their true colors, opting for evenings in with mutual friends or just watching movies and relaxing with a bowl of popcorn. Still, the reluctant Reagan wasn't ready to lock into anything just yet, even with this nice girl from Chicago. Reagan had married Jane Wyman convinced she would be his only wife. When the marriage failed, stranding their adopted son, Michael, and their daughter, Maureen, Reagan was deeply wounded, angry at his wife and himself. He wasn't anxious to be hurt again, but time and Nancy worked their charms.

Reagan finally popped the question on Christmas Day, 1951. A few days later, he called Loyal Davis to ask for his daughter's hand. The couple announced their engagement the next February and were married March 4, 1952. The wedding was not what you might expect of a Hollywood couple. It was a workingman's wedding, very utilitarian: no guests, no press, no family. The "no family" seems odd, but I think Reagan was concerned about having his children there—two kids he shared with another woman. Above everything else, he needed to maintain good relations with Jane Wyman if he wasn't going to complicate his visiting times with Michael and Maureen. The only thing glamorous about the affair at all was the best man: actor and Reagan buddy William Holden. Bill's wife, Ardis, was there, too.

Years later in the White House, I was producing a short campaign documentary for the 1984 Republican Convention. I had come up with what I thought was a good idea to generate a series of still shots for Reagan, showing viewers the many emotions that come with life on the campaign trail. I gathered about fifty photographs of events that had taken place during his first term and had them enlarged. Then I had Reagan sit down across from me and give me a spontaneous reaction to each of them, all while filming his reactions. About two-thirds of the way through, we came to one of Nancy carrying a birthday cake. Reagan immediately said with a big smile, "Oh, I remember that, it was taken at my seventieth birthday!"

"No," I pressed him, "what does this photo **really** mean to you?"

He paused and whispered, "I can't imagine life without her."

He meant it through and through.

Three years earlier, when we were all getting ready to move from Sacramento to Washington, I was with Nancy in their Los Angeles home as she was sorting through boxes and boxes of paper, when I looked up and saw her reading a letter, her eyes welled. Reagan had written it from Arizona, where he was on location for a movie, to their then baby daughter, Patti.

"Dear Patti," the letter begins, "I miss you and Mom so much. . . ." All the rest was a paean to Nancy and everything she meant to him.

Politics and Hollywood have a lot in common. Both are full of phony moments—photo ops, self-serving anecdotes, spin doctoring. I've had my hand in more than a few of them. Believe me, the love that flowed between Nancy and Ronald Reagan was always, always, always the real thing. Even today, when Reagan probably no longer knows he was once president of the United States, the love is still there, undiminished.

The greatest reward of moving to Sacramento and going to work for Ronald Reagan was meeting and marrying my wife, Carolyn. She was a Sacramento girl and actually worked in the governor's two-person regional office in San Francisco—part of a short-lived effort to fulfill a campaign promise to bring the government closer to the people. It's a cliché, but for me it really was love at first sight. Like Reagan with Nancy, I can't imagine life without her. I doubt Carolyn had any idea what was in store for her when she said yes to me, and she certainly knew nothing about the man and woman we both worked for. The San Francisco office might as well have been in Siberia for all the contact it had with Action Central in Sacramento. But Carolyn and the Reagans became friends, too, even though I'm sure there were times when she thought my priorities were reversed.

I'll never forget how excited I was when I told Reagan that Carolyn was pregnant with our first child. As he shook my hand, he said, "Pray that it's a little girl."

It caught me a little off guard.

"What about Ron?" I asked. The Reagans' youngest child had been born years earlier.

"Oh, I wouldn't trade having Ron for anything," the governor said, beaming. "But when you have a daughter, you get to see your wife grow up all over again."

2
NEW MARRIAGE,
NEW JOB

People still tend to think of Ronald Reagan as the actor-turned-president, but he made his last movie in 1964. By 1981, when he moved into 1600 Pennsylvania Avenue, he had been a public political figure for seventeen years, and he had been campaigning across the country for much of that time. A longtime Democrat, he first campaigned for Ike in 1952 and then found common cause with GOP presidential candidate Barry Goldwater during the 1964 campaign against Lyndon Johnson and stumped the country vigorously for him. In 1966, he ousted a two-term governor by a million votes. Four years later, he was easily reelected to the California statehouse. In 1976, he nearly stole the Republican presidential nomination from the incumbent, Gerald Ford. Four years later, he ousted the man who would go on to beat Ford in 1976: Jimmy Carter. Another four years later, Reagan defeated

Democratic challenger Walter Mondale in a historic landslide, winning forty-nine of fifty states and amassing more than 54 million votes—more votes than anyone, anywhere in the world has ever won in a freely contested election.

None of this would have happened without Nancy Davis. Reagan intimates have long known this. As history unfolds, more people will come to fully understand Nancy's role in protecting, guiding, and inspiring her husband. Most important, they will understand how, like many husbands and wives, the pair filled in critical voids in each other's personalities. Unlike Ronald Reagan, though, Nancy was not allowed to make a slow adjustment to life in politics. Instead, it hit her like a brick dropped out of the sky.

Until the campaign for Sacramento, Nancy had been a retired actress and Hollywood housewife, doing her best to raise two children in an often unreal environment. Almost overnight, it seems, she would find herself the wife of probably the most closely watched governor in the country, first lady of America's trendsetting state just at the dawn of the most politically turbulent ten years of our lifetimes.

Stuart Spencer, my oldest friend in politics who guided me in my campaign work before I came to Sacramento, had the best seat in the house for watching Nancy's transition from accomplished actress to seasoned political wife and confidante. Stu signed on with Ronald Reagan back in 1964 when the dust was still settling on the Goldwater-Johnson debacle, and he managed the upset victory over Pat Brown in 1966. Along the way, he also helped the Reagans navigate their way from Hollywood to politics, a seemingly short trip that very few people successfully complete. Stu was my other main tutor in Nancy 101.

From the outset, Stu knew the quiet lady accompanying Ronald Reagan would prove to be very important. He was able to divine on the spot—somehow—that they were inseparable and that Ronald Reagan valued her counsel and trusted her judgment. Like me, Stu formed an important alliance with Nancy, and she increasingly relied on his judgment and advice.

Spencer told me that a few months after meeting Reagan for the first time, he sensed a subtle, yet strong desire to be president of the United States someday. They never spoke of it, but Stu, a great judge of people, said it emanated from the Californian. He didn't get the same feeling from Nancy. His thinking at the time was that Nancy would tolerate one run for office but didn't want to make a life out of it. Privacy was just too important to her, he thought. Almost four decades later, I still agree. All those people who for years wrote that it was really Nancy pushing Reagan toward politics were plain wrong. Nancy wasn't her husband's puppetmaster. To the contrary, she raised serious questions each time he entertained a run for political office and then in the end did whatever was necessary to help him. He's the one who lived and breathed the subject. She went along as and when she felt she had to. The proof, if needed, comes from an unlikely source: Reagan's first wife, the actress Jane Wyman. Wyman's divorce petition complained that her then husband talked about politics at every meal.

As campaign manager, Spencer would spend countless hours with his neophyte client. Nancy would be at his side more often than Spencer expected. He thought she would bore easily at the minutiae of the administrative side of statewide politics, but he was wrong. Nancy was an intense listener. Spencer liked to compare her to a sponge, soaking up every detail she could.

Stu gathered that although Nancy had no problem navigating her way around a Hollywood set or a Broadway stage, she was inexplicably intimidated by the political process that was about to hit her life like the Pacific surf. I'm certain this was one reason for her focus when listening in on briefings, but there was something else at play, too. I have long written about a wonderful Ronald Reagan contradiction: he's shy. Well, so was Nancy in her own way in this new world of politics.

By the mid-1960s, her husband had learned

ways to compensate. Remember, he had already been elected five times running to the Screen Actors Guild, a tough audience to please. Nancy hadn't developed similar skills yet, but she was always a quick learner. Instead of fighting Spencer's plans for Reagan, she decided to let him do his job. Before long, the two had developed a unique relationship, no easy thing to do with a man as impenetrable as Spencer.

"I'd hate to play poker with Stu," Nancy once told me. "I just can't read his eyes."

Stu, too, was learning about the future first couple and how to deploy them to the greatest effect. Thanks to his work as an actor and corporate spokesman for General Electric, and particularly after his speech at the 1964 Republican National Convention, Ronald Reagan was a hot ticket on the California speaking circuit before he ever jumped into a political race of his own. One day, he would be at a prestigious outlet like the Los Angeles World Affairs Council, the next at a Rotary wife's garden party. The problem was that he couldn't turn down an invitation. Maybe he was just too kind to do so, but the practical effect was the same either way: he was running himself ragged and burning up valuable time.

Reagan would drive his maroon Lincoln along the Pacific Coast Highway, trusty dog-eared scheduling booklet at his side on the empty passenger seat, hurrying from pillar to post, with no sense of priorities. Until, that is, Nancy snatched the schedule from her gracious and accommodating husband and began working the phones. Early on in our acquaintance, she told me how she would call each person on the list, grilling them for information about the event or speech, and then dropping the ones that seemed unjustified. She set the bar at a fairly reasonable level: would the speech help Ronald Reagan? If so, great; if not, bye-bye. In her direct, no-nonsense way, Nancy had no problem telling Mrs. McColl what her husband could never do: that Ronald Reagan regrettably would be unable to address her monthly book club gathering. Soon enough, others would be fulfilling this role, myself among them, but Nancy never stopped looking over their (and my) shoulder when the appointment book came out on the table.

People often pooh-pooh the role of scheduler in politics. Even the name sounds petty. But whether it's a small-town mayor or the leader of the free world, the person who controls the schedule has in some ways the greatest potential to do good or harm. Time is the one thing a politician never seems to have enough of, even more so than money. That's why one of the first duties I sought when Reagan won the White House in 1980 was the presidential schedule. Nancy, among others, helped make certain I got it.

During the Sacramento campaign, Spencer

knew that Reagan couldn't do everything on his own. You only have one candidate, he reckoned, and states don't get any bigger than California, so getting Nancy on the road was not only the next best thing; it was critical. Stu approached Nancy and asked her to do some campaign events in the northern part of the state, couching it in terms that her husband was becoming fatigued and simply wasn't Superman. His plan worked like a charm, and the reticent wife hit the campaign trail, doing question-and-answer sessions in tiny hamlets of northern California.

Not that it came easily, even with Spencer's coaching. Sure, Nancy had been in movies, but as familiar as film stars seem to us, they always meet the public with the safety of the camera between them. That's a lot different than hanging around fund-raisers or doing a meet and greet with voters at the local bingo hall. Nancy told me later that the morning after the first political reception she attended with her new candidate-husband, she couldn't move her neck. The doctor who checked her out explained that she had a good old-fashioned case of the jitters. When people are nervous, he said, they raise their shoulders. Couple that with shaking hands for four or five hours, and you've got a first-class recipe for pain.

It wasn't long, though, before Nancy conquered her nerves, got her cues down, and began embracing the Q&A sessions. By the time the 1966 campaign hit full stride, she was another connection to the people for Candidate Reagan— sitting for hours in dusty halls in tiny towns she had probably never heard of before, then briefing Reagan and Stu on the types of questions and gripes the folks were passing on to her.

Of the two, Nancy has always been the better judge of character. Indeed, if Ronald Reagan had a single, great failing, it was always that he was too trusting, to put it diplomatically. He simply had no good "sixth sense" about people or any antennae to detect their darker side. He also had an inability to discipline those who stepped out of line.

Stu Spencer saw this early on, and he knew this was potentially big trouble—on the campaign trail, of course, but even more so if Reagan were to be elevated to high elective office. He decided almost from the start that he would place his chips on Nancy, hoping—praying—that she could fill this critical void. In fact, I think Stu had already learned from friends in Hollywood that she had been doing it for years. As I got to know the Reagans better in those early years, I realized that the governor's reluctance to discipline anyone extended to his children. Nancy had to fill that role as well. Even with her own family, she had to play the heavy, while Reagan remained the guy in the white hat.

Increasingly, she took on the tough jobs that Reagan wouldn't or couldn't handle: particularly staff decisions that were sure to make enemies. Now that I've known Nancy for all these years—and have been at the other end of more than one of her explosions—I can see why she seemed so intimidating to staffers back then. Nancy's style can frighten people. She doesn't like to waste people's time—yours or hers—and she's quick, to the point, and direct in her feelings. People aren't used to that in most enterprises but especially in politics where everyone is so wary of giving offense that most greetings begin with "nice to see you" instead of "nice to meet you" for fear that you might have been introduced before.

Staffers often complained that Nancy was accusatory, but really all she wanted were answers. Yes, directness is off-putting, but so is staff obsequiousness. Nancy never had much tolerance for bootlickers or for anyone who came to a meeting unprepared or just wanted to dance around the issues. Back in her movie days, Nancy had listed some of her pet peeves on an MGM bio sheet: "superficiality, vulgarity especially in women, untidiness of mind and person, and cigars." Not much had changed in the decade and a half before we met. She always sought clarity, constantly asking "why this" or "why that." She was more concerned about getting answers from her husband's advisers than about how she sounded to them. And she still doesn't like cigars.

It amazed me: Ronald Reagan had no problem grappling with the most difficult philosophical issues of our time, but he had trouble dealing with personal relationships. The same guy who would stand tall against the Soviets and never buckle in the face of criticism was incapable of playing it tough with staff. Putting on my shrink hat, I remember the time when Reagan reminisced about his dad limping home deflated after receiving a pink slip from his job of the day. He knew the pain inflicted on a family when a breadwinner was shown the door. I think that, deep in his mind, Reagan didn't want to be the guy to cause that kind of pain. But that left Nancy to do as much as she could from behind the scenes to lift these personnel issues from her husband's usually broad shoulders. They were simply too important to ignore or sweep away.

Sometimes, I would be the heavy; sometimes, Ed Meese or, later, George Shultz or Jim Baker. Sometimes, too rarely, the Boss himself would muster the gumption and tell an underling in his halting way that it was time to say good-bye. Too frequently, the miscreant would be left to twist slowly in the wind until he or she got the message. But more often than not, if Nancy was working the issue, it would be best for all.

Politics, of course, attracts people with supersized egos and all the infighting that goes with them, and the more assertive Nancy became in trying to control those egos and protect Reagan from them, the more flak she drew. Lots of self-appointed VIPs found themselves chagrined that yet another set of eyes was monitoring their daily routines, and being politicians, they couldn't stop complaining to the press about their treatment.

In the beginning, in 1966, Nancy was a regular, if sometimes silent, participant in the many morning campaign strategy meetings. When she did speak up, she would casually mention a conversation with a friend or campaign contributor or perhaps an editorial in a small weekly newspaper. More often than not, her comments would be in the form of a question. Perhaps this was her way of easing into the thick of things, or just a woman's way of inserting herself into a mostly male world. (In politics, too, men are from Mars and women from Venus.)

Over time, Nancy would prove that she knew her stuff even when she failed to turn her husband in the right direction. People forget that Ronald Reagan ran for president four times: 1984, 1980, 1976, **and** 1968. In 1968, Reagan actually considered directly challenging Richard Nixon for the party's nomination, so much so that he accepted a "favorite son" invitation from the California delegation—and, remember, Dick Nixon was a native of the state—to the Republican National Convention in Miami.

The "prairie fire" for Reagan started in the mountain states and spilled over into the Deep South. Inspired by memories of Reagan's stirring 1964 convention speech and dubious of Nixon's conservative credentials, a few of Goldwater's men developed a scheme to try to lure Reagan into the race. I wasn't surprised by the effort, but I was surprised that Reagan was clearly intrigued by the prospect. As the time neared to tip his hat definitively, members of the Reagan team began climbing aboard one by one. Nancy, though, was skeptical from the start. I can still hear her telling Reagan and me that it was "way too early for this kind of thinking."

Unconvinced—or unable to resist the siren song—Reagan allowed the California delegation to do its thing, and the convention turned into a mini-debacle. A seasoned vote counter, Nixon had the delegates sewed up tight in his pocket. After seconding the nomination of the former vice president, Reagan limped back to Sacramento, more than a little embarrassed, to lick his political wounds. For Nancy, the convention fiasco served as confirmation of her own political antennae. After Miami, she would never again hold back her opinion on major political decisions, whatever the Gipper might be thinking; but it was always about protecting her husband, not about driving him on.

In fact, Nancy had serious doubts every time Ronnie ran for office, at both the state and national levels. In 1976, when Reagan was preparing to challenge President Gerald Ford, Nancy was one of the last to be convinced it was a good idea. Her questions were always the hardest for her husband and his top staff to answer. Who is going to organize this thing? Where is the money going to come from? Who specifically in State A or State B will break ranks with a sitting president and support Reagan? Who are we going to put on our board? Do we really have a chance or are we tilting at windmills?

There are also the silly, baseless stories about Reagan getting his conservative views from Nancy's father, Loyal Davis, the Chicago neurosurgeon, or from Nancy herself. That's more tomfoolery. Reagan's views were forged from his soul and tempered by his own experiences. If anything, Ronald Reagan changed some of Dr. Davis's beliefs. Within the Reagan family, it was always "Ronnie" who wore the political and philosophical "pants," not the other way around. The great writer, director, and producer John Huston, a full-blooded liberal, knew Nancy well during her single days in Hollywood. "The idea that Nancy is an archconservative and reactionary and that she is the influence on Reagan and guided his political thinking is absurd, absolute nonsense," Huston once told a reporter. Amen.

Early on, I picked up some valuable clues about how to earn Nancy's trust. It was clear that she was very protective of her husband and wanted to make sure that I had his best interests in mind. I sensed, too, that she wanted to make certain I knew my job was about Reagan, not me. Without saying so directly, I began to let her know I wasn't out to make headlines; my name would never be in the paper. I was happy working for Ronald Reagan and Bill Clark, and I didn't need the recognition.

The relationship I began to forge with Nancy would make me better prepared to serve Reagan later and develop my own political skills. In taking the job nobody else wanted—the guy who, in addition to other duties, would have to answer to California's inexhaustible first lady—I had stumbled upon my niche.

Nancy was soon able to see in me a quality I wasn't at all sure I possessed: the instinct for how the media operates and how to best present Ronald Reagan to it, a job she had been doing alone for years. Although I was admittedly nervous in my initial dealings with her, I think she realized after a few months that she didn't intimidate me. Soon, we were huddling on scheduling, politics, the press, speeches, and other affairs of state. I had fully expected to learn the lion's share of politics at the side of Ronald Reagan. He's the one who bucked the odds and drove California's Democratic machine to the ground. But Nancy proved to be a shrewd political player in her own right.

She forced me to get in front of the governor, promoting issues where Nancy and I found common cause. She also taught me ways to win him over, ones other aides were unaware of. If you want to prevail on Reagan, she advised, never use blatant, crass politics as a tool to pull him in your direction. If I were to say that going to a certain event or supporting a certain bill would mean "political death" for him, he would dismiss my argument out of hand. But if I said that his support of this bill or his attendance at this event would hurt folks or damage a cause, Reagan would want to know more and would often end up taking my side if I could prove my case. Few of even his closest aides in the early years saw Reagan in this light. His most important ally, Nancy, knew this was often the only way to move an inherently stubborn man, perhaps because she had a stubborn streak of her own.

One of my earliest lessons in edging the governor along, Nancy-style, came about a year into

Reagan's initial term as governor when we discovered a pleasant little surprise: a surplus in the California Treasury.

When Reagan was first elected, the state was bankrupt, spending a "million dollars a day more than it was taking in," as Reagan pointed out to anyone who would listen. After taking office, Reagan slashed the budget and reluctantly raised taxes. The strategy worked so well that within a couple of years the state books were back in the black and everyone in the capitol was salivating at the prospect of getting a piece of the pie, mostly in the form of local projects. Every assemblyman who talked with Reagan capped off his presentation by gently hinting to the governor that this would "be great politics."

While Reagan was focused on the discussion, Nancy suggested I slip off and talk with financial chief Caspar Weinberger to learn what he thought should be done with the surplus. "He'll have good ideas," she advised, then went on to explain that this shouldn't be a strictly political decision. We needed to get people involved who could think beyond politics to what was best for the state and its people. It was a good strategy that in other instances would pay off handsomely, but this time, Reagan was already out in front of the first lady.

When the brains finally met on the budget, Cap asked the governor what he wanted to do with the surplus, and Reagan responded, "Why don't we give it back?"

Smiling, Cap pointed out that had never happened before. Reagan said, "Well, they never had an actor for governor before either."

Reagan never once questioned my relationship with Nancy or asked how I was able to get along with her so well. I think he was comforted knowing his wife had a confidant within the inner circle. "Your phone pal," he would frequently say to me, always with affection because he could not think of his wife otherwise.

As for me, I never made a secret about Nancy's and my alliance or my advocacy on her behalf. You would think that other staff might have resented my closeness with Nancy, but to my knowledge, it was never a problem. Bill Clark and Ed Meese, then the legal-affairs counsel, were happy to have me working closely with Nancy because that freed them up to concentrate on policy and appointments. Often, too, they would use me as a back door to the first lady, to get her input on how the governor might react to some new initiative. It was a setup that everybody liked. I also insisted that Nancy Reynolds, the first lady's press secretary and closest staff aide, have an office next to mine, a gesture that elevated the importance of the first lady among the other staff. Reynolds, too, became part of the Reagans' inner circle. Eventually, she and I would accompany the Reagans nearly everywhere they went.

Those early years in Sacramento tested both Reagans, but I think they tested Nancy far more than the Gipper. Unless Reagan's personal integrity was challenged, most insults flowed off him like water off a duck's back. I attribute that to his Midwest upbringing, his rock-solid mother, and his generally good nature. People liked Ronald Reagan. He was disarming and self-assured. Nancy, too, was born with a good heart, but her warmth simply didn't come through the same as her husband's. She didn't come armed with his thick skin.

Chroniclers of human frailty that they are, reporters exploited Nancy's vulnerabilities right from the get-go. While the media attacked the governor's policies and politics, they hit Nancy on a different, more personal level. Instead of shrugging off the press assaults, Nancy would fitfully cancel subscriptions, refuse to watch certain news shows, and blow off social functions if the host or hostess had been critical of her.

Unfortunately, Nancy would sometimes unwittingly arm her opposition. Back then, she simply didn't think much about how her comments and actions might "play" in the press. My life would have been easier if she had, but worrying about such matters wasn't on Nancy's priority chart back then. It was Reagan who mattered first and foremost, and the children after that. When it came to watching out for them, she acted almost out of instinct, often only to find the media shooting back at her.

One of Nancy's earliest clashes came over the governor's mansion. In theory, the mansion should have been one of the spoils of the electoral war that Reagan had waged and won against Pat Brown. In practice, it was anything but. The governor's mansion wasn't just old and drafty; it was a hazard. Nancy had been warned as much by the outgoing first lady. Built in 1877 and probably not touched since, the mansion had been officially declared a fire hazard during the Brown administration. Although the Browns sought funds for years to replace the building, the assembly kept rejecting every new plan as too costly, so the sitting governor of arguably the most powerful state in the land was forced to live in substandard, dangerous housing. The Browns were lucky in one respect: they didn't have any kids to raise in the place. But for the Reagans, it was a different story. Ron Jr. was only eight years old when his dad was elected, and Patti in her teens.

Fearful of piling another worry on her husband's plate, Nancy kept quiet as long as she could, but she couldn't ignore what was right under her nose, and in her ears. The mansion sat downtown right off a busy thoroughfare—"a favorite route for eighteen-wheelers," as Nancy grimly recalls. The semis were so loud that conversations at the family dinner table had to close down until the newest convoy had rolled on by. Zoning wasn't so hot either. Immediate neighbors included a one-star hotel, a VFW hall, and an overused gas station.

For the first few months of Reagan's governorship, Nancy at least had an excuse not to be spending extended time in the governor's mansion. Young Ron was finishing up his elementary-school year in Southern California, and she was down there with him most of the time. Patti was away at school. Nancy's husband, though, couldn't just turn his back on the capital he had campaigned so hard to move to. "I hated to leave him there alone because the place reminded me of a funeral home," Nancy says.

For his after-dinner work sessions, Reagan was forced to retreat from the den to the master bedroom for warmth. The downstairs was so drafty that breezes strong enough to blow papers off the table were a commonplace. One would think perhaps the governor could simply light a fire in one of his mansion's fireplaces, but since the state registered the place as a fire hazard, that was out of the question. For the safety of the chief executive and his family, the house came equipped with a fire evacuation system in the form of a thick rope coiled (loosely) in the master bedroom closet. Although the rope came with no directions, the first couple surmised it was for shinnying down the side of the house in case of a fire. A poor man's fire escape, if you will—**poor** being the operative word.

In truth, Reagan was probably indifferent to the whole situation. He always had a remarkable capacity to shut out peripheral issues when he concentrated, and he was just settling into the biggest job of his life. If the assembly had decreed that he sleep in the back of a Pinto, I'm sure he would have made do. But once Ron Jr.'s school year ended and Sacramento became a more frequent family gathering spot, Nancy's focus inevitably shifted to the place taxpayers expected her to call home for the next four years.

Nancy tried to keep a stiff upper lip, opting to gather intelligence and even talk with the local fire chief. She was particularly concerned about young Ron and how he would escape in case the worst happened. Surely, that rope in the closet wasn't the only recourse! Nancy recalls that she received some interesting advice from the chief: eight-year-old Ron should simply take a drawer out of the dresser, toss it through the double-paned windows, and jump out after it. A broken pair of legs was better than getting burned, the chief concluded.

This little pearl of wisdom brought Nancy not only to tears, but also to the realization she would have to have a sit-down with her husband. Once she framed the issue as a threat not just to him, but to herself and their children, Reagan readily agreed that the status quo just wouldn't do. He would make the necessary calls in the morning. Meanwhile, the first couple would find a newer, safer place to live in Sacramento. Surely, no reasonable person could have qualms with that.

Well, maybe we weren't being entirely reasonable, but the governor's senior advisers had a big qualm, myself included. Moving out of the mansion would look as if the Reagans were too good for the house that California's governor had been living in for decades. The media, I knew, would also paint the Hollywood upstarts as snubbing their noses at history. Firetrap or not, the mansion had been the site of lavish parties for assemblymen, national politicians, and the press for decades upon decades.

Unfortunately, the **Sacramento Bee,** the capital's liberal-leaning guardian, got word of the move almost as soon as Reagan's staff did. My guess is that a fellow staffer was trying to kill the idea before it could be properly conceived. This lifeboat was springing leaks before it even got in the water. Soon, the local graybeards were outraged. Desert the governor's mansion? Why, you would think we had proposed doing away with motherhood and patriotism. They rejected the proposed move out of hand.

Nancy, God bless her, didn't yield an inch. "If they find the house so appealing, let them spend a few nights there," she would mutter to me after some new op-ed column had raked her over the coals. In hindsight, it was a vintage performance. She was so confident of her position—the safety of her family versus the political fallout—that she didn't even consider how the issue would play locally.

Call it naïve, or maybe unfeeling, but these types of potholes are what get you in trouble in the world of partisan politics. It was just the type of diversion her husband didn't need as he was launching a sea change in California politics, but Reagan stood by her like a rock. And for once he had some bipartisan support: a group of wealthy Republicans **and** Democrats bought a brick Georgian on a large lot in a lovely old residential section east of the capitol, rented it to the Reagans for their remaining time in Sacramento, then sold the property off to a new owner after they left. Reagan later said that he knew they had made the right decision when he came home early one day to the new house to see several bikes and toys strewn across the lawn—a sure sign that Nancy had moved them into a kid-safe neighborhood. Ironically, history finally vindicated her, too: a few years afterward, when the mansion was converted to a museum, visitors were not allowed upstairs . . . because it was **unsafe.**

The mansion drama would go on for many more years. Toward the end of Reagan's second term, the state finally approved the construction of a new governor's mansion on a picturesque bluff overlooking the American River. There were two problems, though. The first was that the mansion—designed by a Los Angeles architect—stood out like a sore thumb among the more contemporary, utilitarian homes in the area. It was also way too far away from the statehouse to be remotely practical. Construction took so long that the Reagans never had a chance to spend a night in the mansion. The next governor, Jerry Brown, the son of the man Reagan beat in 1966, could have moved in, but he refused to spend a single night there, opting instead for the floor of an apartment across from the capitol. The state later sold the white elephant, and to this day, the governor of our largest and arguably most important state does not have a formal "mansion."

Being "right" about the governor's mansion, though, didn't grant Nancy any reprieves from the slings and arrows of the media, then or later. While Ronald Reagan went on to become the "Teflon president"—the affection people felt for him was so real and so broadly based that nothing bad, it seemed, could stick to him for long—by contrast, Nancy would become something like the "flypaper first lady." She suffered through more tough press coverage than any president's or governor's wife I've ever known of. To this day, I don't understand the animus the press corps had for Nancy, but I recall vividly one of the earliest profiles of her, a scathing portrait that set the tone for coverage for years to come.

The article appeared in the normally tame **Saturday Evening Post,** in the early summer of 1968. Sardonically titled "Pretty Nancy," it is anything but pretty. The article almost sneers at Nancy for being a traditional wife and mother, someone who had deep-sixed her own ambitions so she could stand by her man. (Worst of all, in the Age of Aquarius, the man she had chosen to stand by was a conservative's conservative.) Nancy's mother would have been portrayed by the same writer as a hero, a single working mother who had tried to do it all, but Edie Davis's daughter had taken the wrong fork in the road of history as far as the reporter is concerned. Feminist contempt fairly drips from every word. Thankfully, the reporter didn't get her hands on Nancy's Smith College yearbook. She would have had a field day with Nancy's proclamation that her greatest ambition was to have a successful, happy marriage.

As unfair and tilted as it is, the article was an effective weapon, a well-placed, well-timed salvo at the new first lady of California. The press had laid down a marker. Amazingly, not until the Reagans went to Washington twelve years later would there be a new national profile on Nancy.

As the so-called guardian of the Ronald Reagan image, I can see now that I should have made the perception of the first lady an equal priority. The real Nancy Reagan was always so much more complicated than the caricature, and probably no one knew that better than I did. But at least in those Sacramento years, there probably wasn't too much anyone could have done. Most serious political reporters at the time were cigar-smoking guys who didn't give a hoot about first ladies, and the women who had made it to the capital as statehouse reporters weren't likely to identify with Nancy Reagan.

The **Saturday Evening Post** article was the first that I can remember in a national publication to ridicule Nancy Reagan for "The Stare," but it wouldn't be the last. Far from it. In Washington, for some reason, "The Stare" was rebranded as "The Gaze," but whether it was the national capital or the state one, liberal pundits and the Democratic political establishment could never stop snickering when they saw Nancy sitting in rapt silence during her husband's speeches. The adoration had to be an act, a woman feigning interest in words that she surely had heard her husband repeat ad nauseum.

The same press that wrote Nancy Reagan watched her husband "adoringly" said that Pat Nixon watched her husband "intently." Well, Nancy did adore Reagan, a statement that I would wager can't be made about a lot of political wives. She also happens to have great big eyes. I'm not sure she was looking any more steadfastly at Reagan than Rosalynn Carter looked at Jimmy or Barbara Bush looked at George, but practically the first thing you notice about Nancy in any circumstance is her eyes. Beyond that, she had then and still has a movie star's presence. People are simply drawn to look at her. Most important, she wasn't just admiring as she listened. She was weighing and evaluating.

If Reagan happened to be delivering a new speech, Nancy was anxious to hear what he had to say, often asking me later for transcripts. She was very interested in policy, particularly her husband's brand of policy. If the speech was an oldie but goodie, Nancy would listen for any tweaks he made to accommodate the audience of the day. Especially early in his political career, Reagan loved to feed off his audience, and sometimes he'd toss out more "red meat" than most listeners could digest. Behind closed doors, Nancy would often serve as a good barometer on how certain lines were likely to play in Peoria and elsewhere.

There was a lot happening behind that "stare," but at heart, the stare was just what it looked like. Believe it or not, Nancy actually did like to listen to her husband's speeches. I probably heard more of Reagan's speeches over the years than even she did, and I enjoyed every one of them, especially the punch lines and other zingers Reagan liked to toss like mini-grenades at scurrying liberals. He always knew how to keep everybody, including his wife and staff, interested in what he had to say.

Today, long after the fact, even some of the Reagans' harshest critics concede that Nancy's onstage affection for her husband was no act. None other than the **Washington Post**'s Sally Quinn recently told **Vogue** magazine that Nancy "got a lot of flak about 'The Gaze.' But now we know it was real." This is a major concession from someone who used to regularly join in on the criticism for readers of the **Post**'s Style section.

Aside from media attacks, politicians inevitably confront criticism out in the public. I'll never forget one unpleasant encounter Nancy told me about that occurred during a flight from Sacramento to Southern California. It was just a few weeks after Governor Reagan had been sworn into office. Nancy was reading a book when she overheard three men in the row directly behind her complaining about the new governor. Between ordering beers and downing them, they skewered Reagan on everything from his budget to his appointments. It was the first time Nancy had ever heard strangers talk about her husband this way, and she was shocked. Surely these people haven't ever met Ronnie, she thought. Nancy festered for a few minutes, then she lost it. She leaned her seat back as far as it would go, nearly putting her head in one of the armchair critics' lap, and let loose.

"That's my husband you're talking about!" she practically shouted. "You don't know what you're saying. He's going on television tonight, and if you watch him, you'll learn the real story on the budget."

You could practically hear the rivets straining in the wings by the time she was through. The stunned threesome kept quiet until they reached the safety of the terminal.

Standing up for her man on the airplane was second nature to Nancy Reagan, but she also couldn't ignore the small taunts and mistruths the press had started lobbing her way.

"When I was in Sacramento," she once said, "I used to go home and take a bath and have imaginary conversations in the tub with people who criticized me. And, of course, I was marvelous!"

• • •

I always find it strange that the Reagans came to be regarded as such a traditional couple, a throwback to another era. Ronald Reagan was America's first divorced president, a dad who, like lots of divorced dads, had plenty of problems with the kids of his failed marriage. One of the most spiritual people I have ever met, he attended church periodically at best. Unlike most politicians, though, he didn't much worry what people would think about that. He knew who he was. Nancy herself was the product of a broken home until her mother remarried. As a mother herself, Nancy never claimed to be perfect—and the Reagans collectively were anything but the perfect family—but it wasn't for lack of trying.

To me, the Reagans always seemed the most modern of couples, even though they clung to the values of the 1950s. Average Americans, I think, understood that. They looked at Ronald and Nancy Reagan and saw themselves: moral but not pious people, a second-chance marriage swimming upstream against the social dislocation of the times. Liberals, of course, saw all this through a different lens, and the more elections Ronald Reagan won, and the more votes he won them by, the more he and Nancy pained their delicate sensibilities.

From the onset, the liberal elites didn't know

what to make of the Reagans. In Sacramento, they were just plain baffled by them. Since the Reagans hailed from Hollywood, people expected them to bring some glamour to the capital overnight. After all, how many times does a pair of actors take over the governor's mansion? Maybe there would even be one of those messy movie-star divorces, or at least pool parties where famous people behaved very, very badly à la the Kennedys. Legislators in Sacramento were used to having after-hours access to a backslapping governor. Heavy drinking, girlies, cee-gars, lots of card playing, and plenty of backroom dealing— they were all part and parcel of the gubernatorial portfolio. No one wanted that to change, and maybe the Reagans could make it even spicier.

At least initially, Nancy couldn't have been more amused by these expectations. She didn't give a hoot about social climbing, and of course she had no intention of being Ron's "ex." Reagan also had no desire to be a business-as-usual governor, during the day or after hours. After all, he reasoned, why should I change my life just because I'm now in elective office? I often think that, of all of us who were along for the ride with the Reagans, the only people who didn't change over the years were the two people at the top: Ronald and Nancy.

At heart, too, the Reagans were anything but nocturnal party animals. Other than the early days of their courtship, their lives were extremely simple. Nancy literally expected her husband to be home every evening for dinner, governor or not. They would eat together, have an after-dinner cup of Sanka—Reagan's favorite coffee—and then he'd retire to his study for an hour or two of executive homework. While the governor labored over his papers and reports, Nancy would help son Ron with homework or join him for television or a board game. It all seems like standard stuff to me, but it left the media and the pols in Sacramento absolutely cross-eyed. Who **were** these people?

Of course, the statehouse press couldn't resist trying to drive wedges between the governor and his first lady. Divide and conquer has always been a good rule of thumb, so reporters and other wags in the capital began murmuring that Nancy hated the ranch time that Reagan loved. As is so often the case, the gossip couldn't have been more wrong. Nancy might have worried more than Reagan about breaking a fingernail while she was riding the range or plastering a wall, but she understood from the beginning how important ranch time was to him, and slowly it became the same for her.

Reagan had already owned a ranch in Malibu when he and Nancy were married. It became a haven for their growing family. Even today, the "kids" reminisce about their times there. Reagan sold the Malibu spread when he became governor—it was too far from Sacramento—but it wasn't long before they were spending weekends looking for another ranch to buy. They settled, so they thought, on a piece of land in Riverside County, but it was an undeveloped tract with no house or infrastructure, hardly the spot where a weary governor could hang his hat and gather with his family. Finally, near the end of Reagan's second term as governor, he found the ranch of his dreams, Rancho del Cielo: 680-plus acres, nestled in the Santa Barbara foothills near the Los Padres National Forest, with a hundred-year-old adobe "shack" and an old barn. It was love at first sight for Reagan and Nancy, and a good thing it was because there was **lots** of work to be done. I remember so many times driving up there, pulling into this little swale where the adobe home was, and seeing the governor and first lady up to their elbows in projects: tiling floors, laying stones for a patio and later building a cover for it, plastering, putting in new windows, you name it. Yes, they had handymen to help them, but both Reagans poured their blood and sweat into that place, believe me.

One of my favorite moments from those early years at the ranch was the time Reagan decided he wanted to make a lake from a little spring that ran near the house. His helpers used a backhoe and plow to dig out the basin, but the lake filled up with black snakes about as quickly as it filled up with water. Undeterred, Reagan waded in up to his hips and began snatching up snakes and stuffing them into a gunnysack. When he was through, he hauled the sack up to the patio to scare Nancy, who couldn't stand snakes, but she had seen him coming and run off to hide.

Later, when Reagan became president, the ranch would become Ronald and Nancy Reagan's real Shangri-la. Sure, they would use Camp David as often as possible—it's only a short helicopter ride from the White House—but it was Rancho del Cielo where they really got away and enjoyed a "home" together.

While Reagan would do his tack room and barn work, his fence fixing and all the other chores of ranch upkeep, Nancy would do her "phone work." Reagan wasn't a phone guy, but Nancy knew things couldn't simply shut down because the Reagans were cloistered at the ranch. She used those quiet ranch weekends to keep in touch with old acquaintances and to reach out to new ones. More often than not, the beneficiary of these chats was her husband, as Nancy would gather intelligence and learn more about the people who had her husband's best interests in mind—and those who didn't.

As Nancy labors behind closed doors today, I know that some of her happiest memories are from the ranch, especially when the two of them would greet the sunset with an evening cocktail—Reagan, a screwdriver, and Nancy with a frozen daiquiri—admiring the bucolic setting and sweeping vistas.

One thing Nancy didn't do at the ranch, by the way, or almost anywhere else was cook. I was amused to find a recipe for "Nancy Reagan's Monkey Bread" in the **New York Times Magazine** while I was writing this book, because Nancy didn't like spending time over a hot stove. Mind you, she could always spot a great recipe. I asked her a few times how somebody could understand a recipe if they didn't cook. "I have a great imagination," she said. And, of course, she had a lot of help in the kitchen.

It was her imagination and staff that made a dinner at the Reagans' a superb adventure. At the White House, Nancy planned most of the formal meals but left the execution and the cooking to the pros. Left to their own devices at the ranch or elsewhere, the Reagans would make a meal of their favorites: macaroni and cheese or barbecue. Comfort foods for comfortable moments and people entirely at ease with each other.

Despite the negative press, there would be opportunities to forge a new image for Nancy. When Reagan took office in 1966, people started asking what projects the new first lady would be taking on. Most politicians' spouses can answer that question in their sleep, but Nancy was still making the transition from actress, housewife, and mother and didn't have a ready answer—another blot on her record. But she knew she liked to help people, especially sick people. She always said that if you feel sorry for yourself, a visit to any hospital would cure you pretty quickly. And so that's what she started doing: visiting hospitals, talking and listening to the patients.

During a visit to the Pacific State Hospital near Los Angeles, Nancy learned about the Foster Grandparents Program, a brainstorm of Sargent Shriver, the Kennedy in-law who had been the first director of the Peace Corps. The program serves as a bridge between two groups of people who have much to give one another: lonely elderly folks and children in need, especially mentally retarded kids. Seniors often have vast reservoirs of patience that can be tapped in dealing with kids who need considerable attention; many of the elderly also feel as if they've hit a wall. Perhaps a spouse has died or their own children have moved away. Foster Grandparents offers them a chance to feel useful again. For their part, the challenged kids respond immediately to the additional doses of love and attention and simple time that the seniors have to give.

From the moment she was introduced to Foster Grandparents, Nancy knew it was a program she could sink her considerable energies into. Soon, she was helping to raise additional funding, both public and private. In time, the program caught the attention of other states and activists, and Nancy helped expand it to include juvenile delinquents, and deaf and blind kids. Nancy said, "It was like watching one of your children grow up to become a successful doctor, helping people everywhere." She still treasures the many letters she received from elderly participants, people who rediscovered a purpose in lives that just seemed to be marking time. Her favorite is from a woman who wrote: "You told us we were important and doing something worthwhile, so we sort of sat back and grinned at ourselves since we're being useful at sixty or eighty. We'll strive now to be even better."

The elderly and the needy kids in the Foster Grandparents Program moved Nancy Reagan deeply, but wounded Vietnam War veterans tugged at her soul. Over all the years I've known her, the most emotional I ever saw Nancy get— outside of family matters—was when she was talking with the heroes who had been wounded fighting for America. She couldn't get their personal stories out of her mind, especially those told by the prisoners of war.

Nancy's interest was first captured by a triple amputee. She was moved when he said that his only regret was that he couldn't go back and join his buddies on the front lines. She was stunned at how the fighting men and the naysayers back home could be at such polar extremes. As she visited and became friends with more and more vets, she began to hear troubling stories about the federal government's real commitment to fighting and winning in Southeast Asia. Many of the vets were bitter that they had been sent into battle without the political will at home to prosecute the war to the fullest extent. She relayed her findings to her husband, who was aghast that the country was tying one hand behind our soldiers' backs.

On Fridays, Nancy began flying early to Los Angeles, so she could head directly to a veterans' hospital in west L.A. She'd literally sit for hours with the young soldiers, their wounds fresh, reading to them, listening to what they had to say, or just holding their hands. Often, she would leave with a promise to call a wife or sweetheart, a task she faithfully performed as soon as she could. Being able to remain composed and optimistic in the face of such trauma was, I think, another benefit of being raised from age eight in a doctor's household. Nancy was Loyal Davis's daughter in more ways than one.

Her work with the vets drew some rare positive media attention, and she was asked to write a weekly question-and-answer newspaper column about military families. Nancy agreed with one stipulation: that her payment be sent to the National League of Families of American Prisoners of War and Missing in Action. She was amazed by the wives who formed the POW/MIA group—at their toughness even when they had no way of knowing if their husbands were dead or alive.

Nancy made sure that she and Reagan were on hand when one of the first planeloads of released POWs landed in California. As they waited on the tarmac to greet the returning men, Nancy held Reagan's hand tightly. She didn't know what to expect. She'd heard so many stories from her wounded vets about the horrors of this war, but she could only imagine the hell these men had suffered in POW camps. Jeremiah Denton, who had spent nearly eight years in prison and would later go on to be elected to the U.S. Senate from Alabama, was the first man off the plane. As she watched him and the others set foot once again on American soil, Nancy was struck by their strength, the crispness of their salute, the pride in their eyes.

"We've got to do something more," she told Reagan.

He agreed, and they came up with a plan to host a series of intimate dinners at the Reagan homes in Los Angeles and Sacramento. Nancy felt that a ballroom simply would not have been the right venue for such a gathering. She insisted the men bring whomever they wanted: wives, mothers, dads, kids. It was their evening.

The first dinner in Sacramento was unforgettable. The men were fresh off the plane; their memories, still raw. You could have filled an aquifer with all the tears that were shed that night. I recall going through two linen napkins as I wiped mine away. Nancy had enlisted other families in the neighborhood to welcome the POWs to the Reagan home. As the soldiers arrived, families stood two to three deep along the Reagans' walkway, cheering the men on. Navy Commander Charles Southwick, who had been held captive for seven years, had a gift for Nancy: the little metal spoon that he had used for every "meal" he was served in captivity. Nancy sobbed as she held it. The tears were just starting to dry when the harrowing tales began. The prisoners told us of the communications system they used to transmit messages between holding cells, essentially a Morse code. Imagine our shock when we saw a pair of POWs embrace in the Reagan living room. They were the best of friends— thanks to the code they developed—but they had never seen each other face-to-face. As soon as they heard each other's name mentioned, they put down their drinks and fell into each other's arms. The smile on the faces of Ronald and Nancy revealed a deeper satisfaction than words could ever describe. Both Reagans wore bracelets bearing the names of men missing in action or known to be in a prison camp. One of those names belonged to a navy aviator named John McCain. To this day, the senior senator from Arizona remains one of Nancy's closest friends.

One dinner in particular is burned into my mind. A young, one-stripe marine escorted his father who had been held captive for years in a tin hut, forced to remain bent over at the waist. He had lost the ability—or the desire—to talk and hadn't uttered a sound since coming home. Gaunt and ashen, he looked confused as his son introduced him to Governor Reagan and Nancy. Some time later, as we all sat at round tables under a large white tent in the backyard, the conversations suddenly ground to a halt when the two hundred guests and returned prisoners realized that this heretofore mute POW was standing and singing "God Bless America." I've never seen such a display of emotion as we all rose to join him in song.

3

WELCOME TO THE MADHOUSE

As people began pressuring Ronald Reagan to run against fellow Republican—and incumbent president—Jerry Ford, Nancy worried. That's how it always has been: Nancy worries, Reagan crusades. The date was early 1975. The Reagans had just moved back to their house on San Onofre Drive in Pacific Palisades from Sacramento. For Ron, the immediate crusade was to make some serious money. His two terms as governor had been a howling political success, but he had bills to pay and a family to provide for, and no one has ever gotten rich off a governor's salary.

I'd gone back to private life, too, but I was still working for the Reagans. Reagan had retained me to help drive up his already high exposure. That part was easy. Soon, the big bucks were rolling in through a nationally syndicated radio show, a newspaper column, and numerous speaking gigs. But everyone knew that, as far as Reagan was concerned, the private sector was only a temporary port of call. There was one more elective office to win, and Ronald Reagan intended to do just that.

The question was when to make the run for the presidency, and that's what made Nancy queasy. Certainly, Jerry Ford was vulnerable. He was filling out the term of a disgraced president; on his own he had never won more than a House seat from Michigan. All that sounded promising, and as Jimmy Carter would soon show, Jerry didn't hold broad appeal for the general electorate either, at least under the circumstances. But Nancy had a way of cutting to the chase. Would the Republican Party frown on this run against Ford? And if it did, where would the funds needed to mount a national campaign come from? As events turned out, they were exactly the right questions to ask.

Reagan and Nancy did decide—together, as they made all important decisions—that Reagan would try to wrest the Republican nomination from Jerry Ford, and once they made the decision, they both jumped into the race full throttle, but it was not to be. The last evening of the 1976 GOP convention in Kansas City, sitting in a box with the Reagans and watching the Fords celebrate, I thought of a classy toast that Nancy had offered to her husband the night before. Reagan was apologizing for not winning and offering his thanks when Nancy stood up and said, "Honey, in all the years we've been married, you have never done anything to disappoint me. And I've never been prouder of you than I am now." The next day on the campaign plane for the last time, Nancy spent the entire trip going down the aisle thanking each staffer and comforting the sobbing ones.

Four and a half years later, of course, it was the Reagans and their supporters who were doing the celebrating. The Iranian hostage crisis had just ended. A decade and a half after he burst into the national conscience with his electrifying speech in support of Barry Goldwater, the ex-actor and corporate pitchman Ronald Wilson Reagan had just been inaugurated as the fortieth president of the United States, and Nancy Reagan, who never aspired to more than being Reagan's wife, was America's first lady.

You would think that being first lady would be one of the plum prizes in the land. In fact, it is one of the strangest positions ever created. Without ever seeking elective office yourself, you're suddenly cast into the national limelight and fair game for late-night shows, comedy-club skits, the gossip columns, and any other dirty and minute dissections of motive and principle the media wants to dish your way. Even in these less deferential days, the presidency comes with a certain amount of built-in respect. But a first lady's job? Good luck.

Dress down too much and you're dowdy (Barbara Bush, Mamie Eisenhower). Dress up too much and you're a queen bee. Fail to smile sufficiently (Rosalynn Carter, Pat Nixon) and you'll be branded a steel magnolia. Smile too readily and you're a Barbie doll. Sit and actually listen closely while your husband gives a speech, and you can rest assured that a Style section mention of "The Stare" and "The Gaze" will be waiting for you with your morning coffee. Hillary Clinton and Eleanor Roosevelt both tried to pitch in on policy matters, and both got labeled a "b" word that rhymes with "witch" for their troubles. (People forgot sixty and more years later how pilloried and adored Eleanor Roosevelt was in her day, in roughly equal measure.)

Normal couples get to have their spats in private. Their coping with problems—drugs, alcohol, their own children, life in general—isn't fodder for the op-ed page. If one of them should stray from their marriage vows, they get to work it out in private, or with the help of a counselor pledged to silence. Not so presidents and first ladies, at least not so long as there are supermarket tabloids and readers who will buy them. And if, perish the thought, your husband should die or be killed in office and you are to remarry—and your new husband happens to be a superwealthy Greek shipping magnate—you will go to your grave as Jackie Kennedy did, accused in certain quarters of violating a national treasure.

To be sure, some first ladies handle the post better than others. As I write, Laura Bush seems to be doing about as well as anyone could do, perhaps because she has the guidance of a mother-in-law who has been there, done that. But being first lady is inherently a nearly impossible position. There's no playbook or set of instructions to tap into when you come to office. A first lady gets staff, of course, but her people for the most part are focused on her incredibly busy social schedule. Normally, they're not political or strategic in nature. Essentially, a White House first lady is on her own. It's like the father who throws his kids off the dock to teach them to swim, with one exception: the first lady has a media corps watching her every minute, just waiting for her to go under.

In the first year or so, Nancy Reagan would wake each day in the White House to an abundance of negative press. The shrill tone was striking. One charming example was **New York** magazine's urbane observation that Nancy "suppresses the little touch of the bitch inside." I remember wanting to write the editor when that one came out, to ask what kind of "little touch" the reporter had inside **her.**

Just weeks after Reagan took office, Nancy casually commented to an audience that she was going to look for ways to tighten the belt on how the first family spends money. The Iran-Iraq War was playing havoc with oil supplies. Inflation was soaring into the double digits. Money was on everyone's mind. It would have seemed strange if Nancy hadn't mentioned it, but she was the first lady by then, a target-in-waiting.

Unable to control itself, United Press International led its March 5, 1981, story in response to Nancy's comment as follows: "Nancy Reagan, who has two out-of-town hair stylists, recently spent a weekend relaxing with her husband in California and attends socials laden with jewelry, says the first couple is making economic sacrifices." Salivating at the prospect of tweaking the first lady, the "journalist" lost all sense of proportion and neutrality, precisely what I had always thought journalism was supposed to be about. Just to make sure no one felt left out, the piece went on to criticize Ronald Reagan's recent trip to California, jabbing at him for taking along a "retinue of aides, security men, and communications gear."

Twenty-five days later, when the president was shot, all that talk of lugging security men and communications gear around with him sounded worse than ridiculous, but even that misses the real issue. Trust me, Ronald Reagan would have preferred to travel alone. He would have driven himself, for God's sake, if anyone had allowed it. Taking three hundred people with him every time he left the White House wasn't his idea. Nor should Nancy have had to go around in sackcloth and ashes to prove that she was concerned about the plight of people with fewer resources than she had. She pays attention to how she looks. That's who she is. But to assume from that that she lacked compassion is not only illogical; it's cruel and unusual.

(I should note here that the media made just as much fun of Jimmy Carter when he carried his own hanging clothes into the White House, just to prove what a regular Joe he was.)

While her husband's approval ratings were going through the roof, Nancy was greeted with the lowest poll numbers a first lady had ever recorded. There was no basement to the grittiness of the coverage. She was Queen Nancy, Fancy Nancy, the Marzipan Wife, Iron Lady, Ice Lady, Nasty Nancy, Dragon Lady, Airhead. I could go on, but you probably get the point. Once-serious reporters developed a side specialty in analyzing the first lady's clothes, her friends, her interest in redecorating the White House, the plates the first family and guests eat off, and on and on and on.

Part of Nancy Reagan's "image problem"—maybe a large part of it—arose ironically from her years as part of the Hollywood Dream Machine, or so it seems to me in retrospect. Before Sacramento, she and Reagan had spent the bulk of their adult years among actors, people whose livelihoods depend on how the media treats them. She knew better than most the way the studios try to manipulate public perception, and she had seen more than one life ruined by the effort to live up to what the studios wanted someone to be. Being Nancy, she had no intention of letting that happen to her once she got to Washington. But Nancy also arrived in Washington with two strikes against her as far as much of the media was concerned. Much as I wished otherwise, that 1968 profile of Nancy just wouldn't go away. It was the well reporters kept going back to when they wanted to build a case against the first lady. Whose fault is that? Well, mine in part. It was inaction by myself and others that allowed that magazine profile to rule the roost as long as it did.

One of the first comments that the **Washington Post's** famous publisher Katharine Graham ever made to Nancy Reagan was, "Just about the only thing I knew about you was that article . . . in the **Saturday Evening Post**." Kay and Nancy would go on to become great friends, but Nancy never mentioned what the **Post** wrote about her and Kay didn't direct anyone to correct some of the mean things her paper wrote about Nancy. They had a healthy personal respect for each other and by and large never discussed "the paper."

To me, the deepest irony of all this is that Nancy Reagan was so often portrayed in the media as calculating. In fact, if Nancy had been a little **more** calculating she could have developed a strategy for dealing with some of this stuff. This was the early 1980s, remember. There were plenty of smokescreens she could have hidden behind: the troubled economy, a restless Soviet Union, the Arabs and the Jews, an unsettled Central America. But hiding was never Nancy's style. Nor was changing her lifestyle to accommodate the carping class or to escape its barbs. Once she got the bit between her teeth, she was gone.

For one thing, Nancy had a new home to worry about. She and Reagan had moved nearly three thousand miles across the country, into one of the signature buildings of the world, and just as happened in Sacramento, the place was a mess. I worked in the White House; I saw what she saw and came to the same conclusion. International landmark or not, the White House in early 1981 was in desperate need of some tender loving care.

Few people have actually been to the White

House residence. I spent a lot of time there with the Reagans, and I can attest to the condition of the place. Cracked plaster walls, chipped paint, beaten-up floors—they were all too commonplace. Some of the rooms hadn't been visited by a painter in probably a generation. And it wasn't just the residential areas that needed work. Even offices within a few feet of the Oval Office were a mess. Many of the building's great treasures—gifts from kings and heads of state, items left by other presidents—had been simply dumped into a storage facility far out on the eastern side of the District. The American people, I feel certain, would have been shocked if they could have seen how this great symbol of the free world had atrophied.

Shocked herself, Nancy sought private funds to restore the White House. All of it was work that any new homeowner would undertake: repair the fireplaces; refinish the floors; paint the walls; replace antiquated pipes, wires, and windows. Sure, the Reagans were only temporary caretakers, but Nancy was going to make sure that the place they would be calling home for perhaps the next eight years was a happy, comfortable place.

To her, seeking private funding just made sense. The economy **was** in the tank, and her husband had been elected in part on the promise to restore fiscal sanity to the federal budget.

What's more, the Reagans—like anyone who can raise enough money to compete in the modern world of national electoral politics—knew people with the wherewithal to get the ball rolling. If Jackie Kennedy had been doing this in 1981, she would have been praised as a pioneer in historic preservation—and rightly so. But as soon as Nancy began seeking donors, large and small alike, she was raked across the coals. The networks led their stories on her effort with film footage of long unemployment lines. How can she use scarce funds for paint and plumbing when people were suffering like this, the message went. What was the first lady thinking of? Well, the future and the past, as it turned out, as well as the present: the White House as history, and as a symbol of hope to so many who have never visited America's shores, and as a home for whatever family the electorate in its wisdom sends to Washington.

Her work was not lost on those who knew best. The White House Historical Association praised Nancy's efforts at rehabilitating the executive mansion, citing "her outstanding leadership in directing the refurbishing of the second and third floors of the White House and for the restoration of its fine arts collection."

The people who donated the money liked what their $800,000 bought, too. In November 1981, Nancy brought a representation of them together, a group ranging from a few little kids who sent in parts of their allowance to the well-heeled types who wrote the checks that put the drive over the top. Afterward, Marianne Smith, a college math professor, explained her motivation to the **Los Angeles Times:** "I saw a newspaper article about the renovation and the impulse to send money came from my heart. It was not a head thing. I thought, here's this nice lady taking on this incredible task, and I sent off a small check, just like I do to the Red Cross, and I couldn't believe it when I got invited here."

A few days after the tour, I was with Nancy when she received her most important review on the restoration. It came from a longtime White House butler who looked Nancy in the eye and said, "Thank you for restoring the White House, Mrs. Reagan. It's beginning to look the way it should again." Nancy beamed the biggest smile I had seen since she'd been in Washington. Alas, the smile wouldn't last for long.

Determined to further restore the White House to some semblance of glory, the first lady next set about replacing the china used for formal "state" dinners where the president hosts visiting foreign leaders. The dirty little secret in Washington is that White House items need to be replaced frequently, not just because of breakage or design but because the people attending events such as state dinners like to carry away the china as a souvenir. A piece of presidential china, after all, is pretty solid proof that you've actually attended a state dinner. The wait staff has watched butter plates, coffee cups and saucers, even uncleared dinner plates being slipped into pocketbooks belonging to some of the bigger names in the world, and never said a word. That's just being discreet, but not surprisingly, this petty theft and breakage take their toll over the years.

By the time the Reagans arrived at 1600 Pennsylvania Avenue, the last full service of china dated back to the Trumans, seven presidencies and many, many purloined plates and cups earlier. To set the table for a state dinner, the White House staff was forced to cobble together pieces of china from different presidencies. Nancy thought this was ridiculous and decided to commission a fine china maker—Lenox, an American company—to come up with some new design concepts. Unbeknownst to Nancy Reagan, a private foundation got wind of her interest in replacing the china and anonymously donated a little over $200,000 worth of new table settings.

As with the rehabilitation of the White House private quarters, no federal funds were used. In this case, the money didn't even come from wealthy contributors who might be suspected of using their contributions to try to gain special access to the president. If ever there was a win-win situation for the people and the White House, you would think this would be it, but the media saw the new plates as another chance to nick the first lady.

Labeling the flap the lowercase "c" "china crisis," the **Los Angeles Times** devoted considerable space to the purchase, reporting such minute details as the fact that "each raised, golden seal in the center of the new Reagan plates will take a minimum of two to three hours to execute by hand." The president didn't escape either. For weeks and weeks, or so it seemed, no press briefing was complete without some guardian of the public good demanding to know if Reagan was going to take his wife to task for her spendthrift ways.

Years later when Bill Clinton was president, Nancy attended Colin Powell's volunteer summit in Philadelphia. All the former presidents and first ladies were there. I was escorting Nancy to a holding room when Hillary Clinton made a beeline to the former first lady. "Mrs. Reagan, I just want to tell you how grateful I am that you bought that set of china. I use it all the time." I couldn't help but think that when she was first lady of Arkansas, she was probably leading the chorus blasting Nancy at the time. Hillary then turned to one of her aides and said, "Make a note: invite Mrs. Reagan to the White House." The invitation never came, and Nancy never went to the executive mansion during President Clinton's eight years.

Then there were the clothes. The first lady had lots of them, and she had a lot of places she had to wear them to. During Ronald Reagan's first term in office, Nancy presided over thirty or more state dinners (and spent almost five hundred hours planning them, in case you're wondering what a first lady does with her time) and another thirty or more dinners that, while official, didn't rise to the level of "state" status. She also oversaw another two hundred fifty or so official White House events—teas, receptions, luncheons, coffees, little parties to honor this person or that.

May God forgive her for it, but Nancy was from the old school. She thought that if you invited people to the most famous address in the country, you shouldn't greet them at the front door in your gym clothes. She also had grown up around the stage and in Hollywood, two venues where a little elegance in dress is part of the air everyone breathes. Some outfits she owned; others she borrowed from designers she admired. The latter were always donated afterward to fashion-design schools.

For a woman of her background, born in 1921 (or thereabouts), dressing to the nines for White House events seemed like nothing less than good manners. But by the early 1980s, Nancy was courting the wrong side of history. Not only had she sacrificed her career to stand by her man; she dressed unashamedly like a woman who had done just that. After briefly entertaining the idea, Smith College, her alma mater, decided against giving her an honorary degree. How to explain it to all those determined undergraduate careerists, walking the campus dressed like peasants, much less to the gurus of the feminist movement?

The press loved piling it on the "foppish" Nancy. Nancy Reagan "has not advanced the cause of women at all," Betty Friedan complained to **Time** magazine. "She is like Madame Chiang Kai-shek, doing it the old way, through the man." Friedan, who wouldn't be caught dead in an Adolfo, had been a year ahead of Nancy at Smith.

Nancy's clothes troubles didn't end at the water's edge, and they didn't start in Washington. I laugh every time I think back to one of my longer "road trips." When Reagan was governor, Richard Nixon often tapped him to represent him abroad. The party's right wing looked to Reagan to keep the wavering Nixon on track, especially on domestic issues like welfare reform. Mindful of that and of Reagan's own growing political strength, President Nixon wanted to keep the Gipper close. One way to do that was to reward him with plum overseas assignments as an official representative of the United States.

The first such trip was to Manila, for the opening of the Philippine capital's new opera house. Staunch U.S. allies during the heat of the cold war, the Filipinos appreciated the presidential gesture and prepared to greet the Reagans with great fanfare. President Marcos and his wife took considerable pride in the construction of the opera house, and Nixon wanted to keep him happy.

The converted military cargo plane we flew in looked great from the outside, with "United States of America" printed boldly along its fuselage. Inside, though, it was stark in the extreme. The Reagans got the only window, a tiny porthole. The rest of us could sit and stare at the cabin wall or retire to bunk beds. Being an official representative apparently didn't guarantee luxury travel. Still, I grew to relish these trips. This one particularly was a small gubernatorial delegation, intimate and manageable enough that I felt comfortable bringing Carolyn along. Before we left, I told the Reagans that we should squeeze a few other stops out of the trip, since we were going all the way to Asia. Nancy agreed, and we put down in Hawaii and Bangkok along the way.

In Manila, Imelda Marcos, not yet infamous,

greeted us with a military delegation. The American ambassador was on hand, and to my great happiness, a few tailors were waiting, too. Knowing Nancy was fashion conscious, the tailors went to work almost immediately, measuring us for traditional Filipino garb that we'd be donning later that evening at dinner. Several meetings later, the Reagans and the rest of the delegation arrived at the hotel to find the fruits of the tailors' labor laid out on our beds. Accompanying directions advised that the dress was mandatory; to everyone's surprise, jewelry was not a permitted accessory. Carolyn was excited as she put on her dress, admiring the craftsmanship and fit. Beaded, with butterfly shoulders, it was identical to all the other dresses prepared for our group—all, that is, except one.

For reasons unstated but easily imagined, Imelda Marcos and her tailors had equipped Nancy with what I charitably called a burlap sack. As demanded, there were no jewels to divert attention from the awful thing. I'm not sure I ever saw Nancy looking worse, certainly not for such a grand event. Nor did it go unnoticed by California's first lady that her hostess, Imelda, looked stunning in a long beaded dress or that she was dripping with pearls and emeralds. Chagrined, Nancy quietly seethed. Never again would she make the mistake of listening to the protocol people or advance guys. She would wear what she wanted, when she wanted.

Looking back, I think the biggest reason for the disconnect between Nancy and the elite media was a simple lack of understanding, on both sides. Sure, the press cut her no slack. Many of them, I truly believe, were offended by the notion of a stay-at-home, traditional wife. But especially early on, Nancy never gave much thought to how to endear herself to the media, and in the information age, that's not a good idea.

Fortunately, Nancy wised up and hired Sheila Tate, a seasoned press hand, before her image problem got entirely out of control. Sheila told me that when she came on board, nearly nine in ten press inquiries concerned Nancy's clothes. Amazing. Together, she and Nancy began looking for ways to go on the offensive without making too much noise or diverting attention from the far bigger battles the president was fighting at the time.

Progress was slow but steady. Then, a little over a year into Reagan's term, Sheila Tate came up with a masterstroke. Her idea was to let the press corps see the Nancy Reagan that the press didn't know: the real Nancy. The vehicle for this would be the 1982 Gridiron Club Dinner, an A-list event where the print press gets together with the political masters of the Beltway to share some laughs and drafts.

The format is essentially a roast: the president is skewered by the press but gets a chance to rebut the genial attacks at the close of the night. Almost always, presidents make sure to attend the black-tie affairs in person, for fear that an absent chief executive will fare even worse than a present one. But showing up wasn't work or duty for Ronald Reagan. He loved the events. I don't think he and Nancy missed one in their eight years in Washington. Because of his time in Hollywood, Reagan was a virtual gladiator in such friendly fights, surviving attacks from the world's most skilled roasters—comedians like Bob Hope, Don Rickles, and Dean Martin. Reagan savored the challenge and knew this stuff. Nancy hadn't been tried in the same venue. Any attempt to inject her directly into the Gridiron affair was going to be risky, but that's exactly what Sheila proposed to me in the early spring of 1982.

Tate knew that, in Washington, they love to kick you when you're down. After the beating Nancy had been taking in the press, the Gridiron wise guys were sure to have something in the evening's arsenal pointed directly, mercilessly, at the first lady. To counter them, Sheila outlined a surprise skit Nancy herself would perform at the roast—a routine that would lambaste . . . Nancy Reagan.

Through a sympathetic Gridiron source, we were able to find out what was in store for Nancy at that year's dinner. Somebody was going to perform a song poking fun at (what else?) Nancy's fashion sense and expensive tastes. Instead of striking back at the press, the first lady was going to go along with the gag and extend it even further to make fun of herself. And to be certain she got the tone and words right, Nancy pulled in veteran Reagan speech man Landon Parvin to help craft a suitable response.

Nancy was able to keep everything—and I mean everything—about that evening a complete secret. Even her husband didn't know anything. As for me, I was girding myself for a tumultuous evening, nervous that Nancy might have bitten off more than she could chew.

Nancy and the Gipper were sitting side by side at the head table, enjoying the meal when the press unleashed its expected barrage at Nancy. A singer pretending to be Nancy Reagan stood before a large rack of clothes, belting out the old standard "Second Hand Rose," updated for the occasion:

Second hand clothes.
I give my second hand clothes

To museum collections and traveling
  shows.
They were so happy that they got them
Won't notice they were ragged at the bot-
  tom.
Goodbye, you old worn-out mess.
I never wear a frock more than once.
Calvin Klein, Adolfo, Ralph Lauren, and
  Bill Blass.
Ronald Reagan's mama's going strictly first
  class.
Rodeo Drive, I sure miss Rodeo Drive.
In frumpy Washington.
Second hand rings.
Donate those old used-up things.
Designers deduct them.
We're living like kings.
So what if Ronnie's cutting back on welfare.
I'd still wear a tiara in my coifed hair.

Like everyone else in the room, I was laughing so hard that I almost missed Nancy slipping away from the head table during the early part of the skit. Reagan, I saw, looked perplexed for a moment but refocused on the singing impersonator. Sheila Tate, who was sitting between two ink-stained, crusty newspapermen, overheard one of them say to the other: "Mrs. Reagan just left. I bet she's really pissed."

Little did they or almost anyone else in the

cavernous room know that Nancy had smuggled in a costume and was donning it in secret while her doppelgänger finished up the song. As the would-be Nancy Reagan departed the stage to well-earned laughter and applause, there was a rustle in the rack of clothes that stood in the backdrop. Then, suddenly, the clothes parted and out came the real first lady dressed, as she put it, as "a bag lady on Halloween."

Nancy had chosen the right description of her little ensemble. At first, even I didn't recognize her. I don't think anybody did. As the guffaws gave way to utter silence, the bag lady began to sing:

I'm wearing second hand clothes
Second hand clothes
They're quite the style
In the spring fashion shows.
Even my new trench coat with fur collar
Ronnie bought for ten cents on the dollar.
Second hand gowns
And old hand-me-downs
The china is the only thing that's new.
Even though they tell me that I'm no longer
**   queen,**
Did Ronnie have to buy me that new sewing
**   machine?**
Second hand clothes, second hand clothes,
I sure hope Ed Meese sews.

The old gal pulled it off, earning a standing ovation even from Ed Meese, whom you would never want to trust with a needle and thread. The crowd yelled for—and received—an encore, and the next day's **Washington Post** fairly smiled with appreciation for the first lady's self-mocking parody.

The skit paid off not just in the capital. Bolstered by the warmer coverage, Nancy felt more comfortable elevating her profile to do good works. Soon, she was traveling around the country, speaking against teen drug abuse. She cut several public service announcements and even spoke to the United Nations about the drug scourge. Nancy understood—for the first time in her life, I'm sure—that she could influence events and impressions on her own. It was the hard way, but Nancy had just learned the first rule of public relations: nobody is going to change your image; you have to do it yourself.

In truth, I'd been somewhat surprised when Nancy took up drug abuse as a cause. Typically, first ladies focus their energies on soft issues like children's literacy and reading—"motherhood" subjects that 98 percent of the electorate can get behind. Their staffs, and the presidents' staffs, like to push first ladies that way, into areas that aren't booby-trapped with political, budgetary, or ideological implications that can cause troubles four years later when the reelection machine cranks up.

Considering what our society was like in 1981, illegal drug usage was anything but a "motherhood" subject, but, as usual, once she had made up her mind, Nancy was not to be deterred. One of her intimates told me that Nancy had been deeply saddened by the overdose death of the son of Hollywood friends, and I also recall how moved she had been by a 1980 campaign visit to a New York drug-treatment center.

Until that moment, Nancy had been mostly insulated from the worst ravages of drugs. Now, she told me, "I was stunned to find out just how large the problem of drug abuse really is." She was impressed as well to see young folks rising from rock bottom, "climbing out of the mess they had made of their lives because of their dependency on drugs." Just as the wounded Vietnam War vets had stirred her to action in California a decade and a half earlier, so she was driven on by these men and women wounded by heroin, cocaine, and the rest of the drug dealer's arsenal of poisons.

Early in the first Reagan administration, Nancy convened a rump group of staff and friends to talk about the best ways to help use her new position to stem the rising tide of drug use. Her staff cautioned her that she was walking into dangerous political territory. At the time, the Republicans were seen as the party that wanted to take the fight to the suppliers—the drug lords and other growers, domestic and abroad—while the Democrats painted themselves as the more compassionate party, believing treatment programs were the preferred solution. Both approaches had merit, in my view, but the chasm between them seemed to widen by the day. By joining this highly charged debate, Nancy risked opening herself up to attacks from both the right and left. But Nancy told me that she saw drug use as a pox that crossed all lines—geographical, racial, political, and economic. It touched everybody, everywhere, somehow or in some way, and that was enough for her.

It was enough for the president, too. He would be the one who would ultimately suffer if the electorate decided his wife was playing politics with people's misery and lives, but he stood by her foursquare. Nancy and Nancy alone would have to decide how best to use the bully pulpit she was inheriting. And did she ever. During her eight years in Washington, Nancy took her crusade to sixty-five cities in thirty-three states, to the pontiff's side in Rome, and to capitals the world over. To spread the message even more broadly, Nancy played herself on an episode of the sitcom **Diff'rent Strokes**, did a onetime stand as cohost of **Good Morning**

America, and narrated an antidrug documentary for PBS.

She didn't stop when the camera lights turned off, either: only recently, since she has turned most of her attention to her ailing husband, has Nancy left it to others to carry her "Just Say No" message forward. And as with the veterans in California, she was never afraid to get involved at the ground level.

One evening after a quiet dinner in the White House residence, Nancy took a call from the switchboard. The receptionist said that a woman from Texas was on the line and that she needed help with a son whose drug use had gone over the edge. Rarely, if ever, does an unsolicited call to the White House get through to a president or a first lady, especially when they have retired to the residence, but the receptionist said that the woman from Texas was in a panic. Unable to resist such a direct plea for help, Nancy took the call.

The Texas woman was nervous but spoke clearly and quickly, anxious to get in her say before the first lady changed her mind about taking the call. Her son, she said, had gone off the deep end—drugs were going to kill him, maybe by his own hand. The mother had hit the point of desperation. She had heard Mrs. Reagan talk about the scourge of drugs. Could she help? Nancy listened patiently, then motioned for a pen to Sheila

Tate, who had dropped by the private quarters. She wrote down the woman's name and phone number and promised to get back to her. Immediately after hanging up, Nancy began digging through an accordion file folder, searching for the name of the head of the Texas Just Say No movement, a man she had met just a few days earlier.

I can only imagine his surprise when he realized that the first lady was on the line, but after exchanging small talk, Nancy got down to business. She conveyed what the woman had told her about her son and her despair, then ended by telling Robby that the boy "needs help tonight."

"Absolutely, Mrs. Reagan," he responded, "I'll call her first thing in the morning."

"Robby, you don't understand," Nancy said with a deft but firm touch, "this has to happen tonight. I really don't think there is a tomorrow for these people."

The phone line was silent until Nancy spoke again, this time leaving no room for misinterpretation: "This lady is not going to spend another night going through this hell."

The Texas Just Say No people did call the woman that night, and they continued to reach out to her and her son in the weeks and months ahead. Nancy kept close to the situation, too. She was thrilled to get word a year later that the boy's treatment program appeared to have been a complete success.

Was Nancy's Just Say No program a success? Plenty of anecdotes like the one above tell us that the answer is a resounding yes, but to get the big picture, I went to an unimpeachable source, one whose opinion would be free of the taint of politics: Joseph A. Califano Jr., secretary of health, education and welfare under Jimmy Carter and now president of the National Center on Addiction and Substance Abuse at Columbia University.

"Did she make a difference?" Califano says. "Without question she made a difference; just look at the numbers before she started and the numbers after."

Just Say No will never be fully appreciated, but the people on the inside know the good the program has done. I was having lunch with Nancy in the early spring of 2002 when a fellow diner asked if he could interrupt. He came offering his thanks for Nancy's work on the antidrug campaign and identified himself as a television producer who had been involved in the **Mike Hammer** series that was popular when Reagan was in office in the 1980s. The show's star, the talented Stacey Keach, had been arrested in London for possession of cocaine and was having a heck of a time maintaining his job as Mike Hammer. As Keach made his comeback, he worked with Nancy to help erase stigmas, demonstrating there are second chances, even in Hollywood.

Califano calls Lady Bird Johnson's beautification initiative and Nancy Reagan's Just Say No campaign the two most productive first lady projects in modern history. The secret of Nancy's, he says, is that it was built on a basic but critical foundation: parents needed backup, and "Nancy filled that role as a 'national parent' when it came to drugs."

I can remember critics calling the campaign simpleminded, especially in its first years. (I also remember the "critics" on the left who seemed to think that "Just Say Yes" made a lot more sense.) But Joe Califano says that it was the very simplicity that made the difference. Saying no was something even a desperate user could try to grab hold of.

"Keeping it simple is why it worked so well," Joe told me. "Nothing's worked as well since. We've had a lot of peaks in drug use and not enough valleys. Thanks to Nancy Reagan, the valleys were not as deep."

Nancy and Califano didn't meet until the mid-1990s when he was drumming up support for his National Center on Addiction and Substance Abuse. She loved his ideas and nearly jumped out of her chair when Califano offered her a seat on the board. "In five years, she never missed a meeting," he said.

As the first lady began to slowly chip away at the icy image the press corps had created for her, I could see her skin growing thicker. Early in the first term, a blistering op-ed column by Rowland Evans and Robert Novak had driven her to despair. Years later when another tough article appeared in a different paper, erroneously quoting Ronald Reagan telling his wife to "get off my goddamn back," I prepared for a deluge of Nancy tears. This was the Iran-Contra scandal, and she had, in fact, been riding Reagan hard. He tended to see the backlash to Ollie North, John Poindexter, and the others in political terms: it was all about liberals trying to bring him down. Far more practical, Nancy kept telling him that, whatever the motivation, the scandal was bleeding his administration dry and he had to deal with it.

Where the reporter got his "goddamn back" line from, I'll never know. Supposedly, Nancy was pressuring her husband to dump Don Regan, but Ronald Reagan would **never** say that to Nancy. Still, the reporter had the kernel of a truth, and I thought Nancy would take it hard. Instead, she was a rock. "That's okay," I remember her saying, "they need to write something every day, don't they?" That was quite a sea change, and to me, it all traced back to the Gridiron skit and the confidence it had given her.

The flap actually points out a big difference between the two Reagans. Averse as he is to confrontation, Reagan would let things slide and slide, hoping for some sort of miracle resolution, while, as I've said, Nancy's reaction to any adversity, any unpleasantness, is to confront it head-on. Sometimes that means confronting it head-on emotionally first. Other than a few occasions, I never knew if Ronald Reagan was really mad or upset; he would try to choke his feelings down and say nothing. Not so Nancy. She lets loose what's on her mind and in her heart. If she has a grievance with someone, you can pretty much bet that she'll take the problem directly to the source. If she regards you as a friend, you can always talk it out over a cup of coffee. After that, it's water under the bridge. End of story.

It was easy for me to tell when Nancy was frosted at me. If I hadn't fielded a call from her in twenty-four hours, I knew something was rotten in Denmark. Careful not to let things fester, I would instinctively pick up the phone and give her a call. "Do we have a problem?" If she said yes, I'd hang up the phone and head straight over for a chat. Sure, we'd argue, but she wouldn't let me leave without a hug.

Most of the time, I didn't have to wait a full day to learn I was in the doghouse. From the very beginning of the Reagan presidency, I had been granted special access at the White House, both to the working areas and to the family quarters. I remember the very first day with Ronald Reagan in January 1981. He asked me where my office was going to be. At the time, I had absolutely no idea, so he walked across the Oval Office, opened the door to the well-appointed study that serves as the president's working office, and told me to move my stuff in there. I was aghast, but delighted at the same time. Noticing my bemused expression, Reagan said, "Look, Mike, I've been trying to get this nice round office all these years. What the hell would I want that little square one for? It's yours."

With special access, though, came special responsibilities. That "little square" office was where I fielded innumerable tough calls from Nancy, most often over the president's schedule, because Nancy's first priority then and now has always been Reagan's health. People forget, myself included, that Reagan turned seventy a month after he took office for the first time. At a time when many seniors are winding down on the golf course, Reagan was just gearing up for the toughest eight years of his life. Even after the president was shot—or maybe because he seemed to recover so effortlessly from being shot—it was easy to forget his age because of his unmistakable vitality, but Nancy would never forget.

"Mike, I just received this week's schedule, and I want to know what you think you're doing over there. My God, you're going to kill him!" she told me in one memorable phone conversation. Point taken, Nancy. If first ladies should be heard on anything, it's on matters like this.

Try as I might to be sensitive to the president's age—and even knowing that Nancy was always waiting at the other end of that phone—I still overbooked Reagan more often than not. There are so many demands on a president's daily life, so many people wanting their two minutes of phone time with him or five minutes of face time. Even for someone like me, who had been parsing out his time since Sacramento, it was almost impossible not to cram his schedule. No one in the world is in demand like a sitting American president. When I overdid it beyond any reasonable bounds, Nancy would always let me know, in straightforward language, that I had crossed the line.

After one of our more candid phone conversations about Reagan's schedule, I opened my office door and walked into the Oval Office,

1.

2.

3.

4.

5.

6.

7.

8.

9.

10.

11.

Welcome Home NANCY

12.

13.

scratching my head, trying to figure out what to purge. The president was leaning back in his leather chair, reading a briefing paper. He looked at me and winked, silently inviting me to unburden myself. Generally, he sided with me on these types of disputes, even though he understood and appreciated his wife's motives. "Mike," he cracked on this occasion, "Nancy can tear up when the laundry goes out."

Nancy's penchant for action sometimes spilled over more directly into politics, never to push her own agenda but to make sure her husband's wasn't slighted or ignored. I remember the time that a western Republican senator who was very close to Reagan failed to support him on a major piece of legislation, raising the possibility of a rare Hill loss during the first term. That evening at some social function, Nancy gently pulled aside the lawmaker's wife, telling her there was something she had to "get off her chest" about how the senator was treating Reagan. Within an hour, Nancy received a call from the wayward senator himself. The next day, he was back squarely in the Gipper's camp.

As I mentioned earlier, Nancy was a stand-in for the Reagan unable to deal with personal relationships. She was the anti-Reagan when it came to seeing the truth in people. Reagan needed only a simple apology to turn the other cheek, even if someone had blatantly tried to screw him over. Nancy cared too much about her husband's legacy and his place in history to let people off the hook so easily. When I say that I don't think the Gipper could have made it to the White House without Nancy, it is the personnel issue that is foremost in my mind. She provided her husband protection from men with less than noble ambitions—a fact that even she is willing to admit.

"Ronnie can be too trusting of the people around him," she once told me, a classic bit of understatement. Another time, she told a reporter, "I think it's the eternal optimist in him, his attitude that if you let something go, it will eventually work itself out. Well, that isn't always so."

I remember huddling with Nancy right after Reagan's own budget director, David Stockman, stuck a knife between the president's ribs in an interview with the **Atlantic Monthly.** Worried that Reagan's economic revolution might never round the corner, Stockman laid down his own covering fire by essentially calling the plan he was hired to implement a joke. Nancy called me after reading the piece, and I approached Reagan to discuss firing Stockman, but the president wouldn't budge. For some reason, he saw something in the young budget chief and wanted him around, and once he had made up his mind, he was stubborn as a mule.

Nancy lost that one, and I did, too. For his loyalty, the president was rewarded with another dagger in the back a few years later when Stockman panned the boss in a book about his White House years. Our consolation was that, despite a huge press run, Stockman's book had miserable sales. Like the media, the publishing world had miscalculated Ronald Reagan's appeal.

Nancy was more effective in helping clean up the Iran-Contra mess. It was a classic example of how Nancy employed third parties trusted by Reagan to help straighten out something gone seriously off track.

Nancy knew long before her husband that because Iran-Contra happened on his watch, Chief of Staff Don Regan would have to go. He simply wasn't the kind of top aide Reagan needed. I had just left the White House, but Nancy asked me to gather a select group of outsiders to talk to Reagan. I immediately went to Robert Strauss, the legendary Democratic wise man, and William Rogers, former secretary of state for Richard Nixon. Since secrecy was paramount, the three of us entered the White House through the Treasury building and used the underground passageway. It is an unknown but fascinating part of the White House complex built during World War II as a bunker for the president and his key staff. As we passed through the long underground halls, you could see rooms of bunk beds and a temporary hospital still maintained in case of a national emergency.

When we arrived, Nancy led us into the sitting room of the private quarters. Reagan was, of course, polite and listened to us earnestly. Bill Rogers said little if anything, but Strauss was very forthcoming. He told Reagan that he was once asked by President Lyndon B. Johnson about his thoughts on the Vietnam War. Strauss responded by telling LBJ exactly what he thought he wanted to hear. He told Reagan that as he left the White House, he felt soiled and vowed that if any president "was stupid enough to ask my opinion again, I would tell him the truth." He then told Reagan that he needed to take a decisive step. He had to let someone go, namely, his chief of staff. Reagan listened somberly and gave no indication about what he thought of the advice.

Strauss told me afterward he thought he had been tough, maybe too tough. But he was assured later when, after he returned home, Nancy called and said, "Thank you, Bob. That was what he needed to hear."

Interestingly, after Don Regan left the White House, he wrote a book that was tough on Nancy (more on that later), and became a celebrity in the mainstream press. But Nancy didn't hold a grudge against Regan. She would later invite him twice to speak at the Ronald Reagan Library, and when he was diagnosed with bone cancer in 2002, Nancy wrote him about her concern for him and his wife, Anne.

While Nancy may have forgiven Don Regan, the same cannot be said for the Iran-Contra scandal's brainchild, Lt. Col. Oliver North, then serving on the National Security Council in the White House. Call me cynical, but I could see North coming a mile away. He was Eddie Haskell in marine's garb. Like most military people assigned to the White House, he was sharp as a tack, but North differed from his contemporaries in the way he worked the president. Where you would get crisp briefings or "yes, sirs" and "no, sirs" from most military officers, North knew how to push Reagan's buttons, playing on his emotions and patriotism. As deputy chief of staff, I made sure that North was never with the president alone.

Nancy was concerned about North, too, and understood my desire to set up a firewall around the Oval Office. And she never forgot how he tarnished her husband's legacy. In 1994, Ollie North had pulled dead even in his U.S. Senate race with Virginia's once-popular Democratic incumbent, Chuck Robb. Momentum was clearly on the upstart's side until Nancy, doing a rare public question-and-answer session, was randomly asked her thoughts on the North candidacy. Usually, of course, Nancy demurs on political questions, especially ongoing campaigns. This time, she didn't. "North almost ruined my husband," she answered, and with that, Ollie North sank in the polls, never to recover. I never understood the power of Nancy's words until, in 2002, a former Robb campaign official told me over lunch that as soon as the campaign got word of the former first lady's quote, the entire Robb staff "did high fives all the way down to Richmond."

There was one staff problem that Nancy did not get involved in, and we all suffered for it. During Reagan's first term, there was an internal battle royal happening right under his nose, yet he refused to step in. In one corner stood Chief of Staff Jim Baker and me; in the other, Ed Meese and Bill Clark, my old boss from the governor's office and the White House national security adviser. Without getting into details, it's safe to say that things were getting pretty ugly, yet the president, as was his habit, refused to address it. Finally, one day I confronted him with the situation.

"Mr. President, you understand that your staff is coming apart, don't you?"

He gave me a reassuring smile and said, "Oh,

don't worry about that stuff, Mike. The media's trying to make hay out of it."

I assured him that no, it was not the fault of the national press corps. Relying on my nearly twenty-year association with the man, I told him as firmly as I could that he must do something.

"I suggest you pull all four of us into the room and call us onto the carpet," I urged him.

"If you think that'll help, let's do it," he said.

A few days later, Baker and I stood across from Clark and Meese. The president quietly paced. The tension was palpable. Nobody would utter a word.

Finally, I said, "Mr. President, I assume that you've called us here to straighten out this little problem we're having."

"Mike, are you saying we have some things to work out here?" Reagan said as if the thought of conflict had never crossed his mind.

Needless to say, Reagan didn't call us onto the carpet—he just couldn't do it—and things went downhill from there.

Meese ended up leaving the White House to be U.S. attorney general; Baker went off to head up Treasury; Bill Clark moved a few blocks to the west to become secretary of the interior. I hung around another year, but that day in the Oval Office, the Exit sign started to shine more brightly than ever before.

• • •

With personnel and most other issues, Nancy and I usually agreed. But we had our share of differences during our long friendship, especially when she felt I wasn't carrying my load when it came to protecting Reagan. Two of the worst moments between us are burned into my mind. I've written about both before, but the stories bear repeating here. The first was the time the Reagans fired me. Or maybe I quit.

A few days after Thanksgiving, 1979, Nancy phoned to ask if I could stop by their Pacific Palisades home for a meeting. The 1980 Republican National Convention was eight months away, and the first primary just around the corner. Reagan was the front-runner for the nomination, but in politics, you can take nothing for granted.

The old Sacramento gang, myself included, had been reassembled for the effort, supplemented this time by a group of well-regarded "easterners"—John Sears, Jim Lake, and Charlie Black. We were very sensitive to the fact that the eastern establishment still dominated elite thinking in America, and Reagan was never its ideal candidate. Sears especially would give us an in with the East Coast graybeards, we figured. He had worked for Nixon and was considered a political genius by the national media. (Sears did nothing to discourage the belief, I should add—he could schmooze with the best of them.)

Inevitably, bad blood had broken out between the old gang and the newcomers. Sears began by driving out Lyn Nofziger, who had been Reagan's press secretary through both terms as governor and then had taken on the thankless task of heading the fund-raising effort for the 1980 campaign. With Lyn gone—and ignoring his advice that I was digging my own grave—I took on the fund-raising job myself.

If I thought at all about why Nancy had asked me to drop by, I figured it was to discuss the money: How much did we have? What were we doing to get more? George Bush, John Connally, and Howard Baker had all thrown their hats in the ring. We worked for every dollar. Carolyn had some errands to run in the general area, so I had her drop me off at the Reagans' that evening in November. She said she would be back in maybe an hour and a half. No problem, I answered. I could always do a little schmoozing of my own if the meeting broke up early.

My expectation of a pleasant meeting pretty much evaporated when Nancy met me at the front door and gingerly asked if I would mind waiting in the bedroom. I was stunned.

"The bedroom?" I asked.

She assured me that it'd be just a few minutes,

but as I walked past the living room on the way to the bedroom, I saw Reagan huddled with the easterners and had my first glimmer that the long knives might be hiding just under the coffee table. I paced the bedroom floor and flipped through an old **Reader's Digest** for twenty minutes and then just couldn't stand it anymore. I was never excluded from these types of meetings. What's more, Nancy rarely sits in on one of them if I'm not there, too. Worst of all, I'd been the one who finally convinced the boss to bring on Sears and company. This was my thanks?

Having worked myself into a fine lather, I stormed out of the bedroom and into the living room. "What the hell is going on?" I demanded.

Everybody looked at the floor sheepishly as Reagan spoke.

"Mike, the fellas here have been telling me about the way you're running the fund-raising efforts, and we're losing money," Reagan said. He went on to expand the brief, but I didn't need to hear more. The Sears crew had clearly forced Reagan's hand: them or me? And he'd made his choice.

"You need to put somebody in charge," I said to Reagan as I turned on my heel, "and if these guys are going to sink to these tactics now, what would we do if we ever got to the White House? I'm leaving."

Reagan followed me out of the room. "No,"

he said, "no, this is not what I want." Without breaking stride—or turning around—I told him, "Sorry, but it's what I want."

Nancy looked just as aghast as he was as I reached the front door, opened it, and stepped into the California air. I took a deep breath, said good-bye to all that had been between Nancy and Reagan and me . . . and then realized I had no way of getting home. Carolyn wouldn't be back for more than an hour. If I had painted my face, put on a bright orange wig, and walked out the door on stilts, I couldn't have made a more clownish exit.

I quietly opened the front door again and found Nancy pacing the foyer alone, clearly upset. Reagan was talking loudly in the living room. I put my finger to my lips, seeking Nancy's silence, and she nodded just as her husband said, "Well, I hope you're happy; the best guy we had just left."

In that moment, I'm sure Nancy fully expected me to ask for her behind-the-scenes support in getting my job back. When I asked instead for the keys to the Reagan station wagon so I could get back to my L.A. apartment, she handed them to me quietly. She had no idea what to say. A few weeks later, the Sears team laid an egg its first time out, losing Iowa to a surprisingly well-organized George H. W. Bush.

Not surprisingly, it was Nancy who finally

convinced Reagan that it was time to purge the easterners and get back to basics with the old California crowd. She could see the toll that the constant bickering and finger-pointing were taking on the candidate, physically and in terms of lost votes. By the time I rejoined the campaign in June 1980, things were safely back in hand. I flew with the Reagans that day to the next campaign stop, then joined them in their hotel suite for a drink after the day's events were over. They were friendly, as if nothing had ever happened, and I decided to leave it at that. During our conversation, I referred to Nancy as usual as "Mrs. Reagan."

"Mike," she said, reaching over to me, "isn't it about time you called me Nancy?" It was enough of an olive branch for me.

The second great rift between Nancy and me was worse because I really had screwed up this time.

It was 1985 and I was arranging a state visit to Germany. Reagan had accepted an invitation from Chancellor Helmut Kohl to participate in ceremonies marking the fortieth anniversary of the end of the European war. Both men rejected the idea of doing an event at a concentration camp. They wanted to stress hope and reconciliation, not the horrors of the past. I also knew that Reagan's emotions were likely to betray him in such a setting. Unlike Nancy, who could light

up a room filled with ailing veterans, Reagan frequently lost his composure in settings that
evoked pain and suffering. Part of my job, as the
one in charge of handling the advance work for
the entire Germany trip, was to find a more suitable venue—some place where the two world
leaders could lay a wreath to commemorate the
war dead.

Along with the U.S. diplomats on the ground
in Germany, I picked what I thought was an ideal
site: a cemetery called Bitburg that couldn't have
looked more picturesque under its beautiful coat
of snow. By now, I had been doing this kind of
work for a long time: I knew what questions to
ask of our German hosts, and I was assured that
no embarrassments were waiting beneath the
winter snow. Little did I know that several dozen
Nazi war criminals were interred at Bitburg, hidden under unremarkable gravestones marked
"SS Waffen."

Anyone who was old enough to watch the evening news in 1985 will remember the rest: as
soon as the word about the Nazis surfaced, all
hell broke loose. In Europe, America, and the
Soviet Union, the outcry was immediate and bitter. Wounds that never quite healed were split
wide open again. World War II veterans marched
in angry protest and sent their medals to the
White House in embarrassment. Jewish groups
demonstrated, demanded, then begged the pres-

ident to reconsider the visit, but as usual when his back was to the wall, Reagan wouldn't budge.

Nancy was furious—at me, of course, for selecting Bitburg; at Reagan for not reconsidering; but even more so at Helmut Kohl for refusing to change the location or cancel the visit altogether. She lobbied me, Secretary of State George Shultz, and anyone else who she thought might be able to put the arm on the German chancellor, but the old burgher was as stubborn as Reagan. When Holocaust survivor and Nobel Prize winner Elie Wiesel came to the White House for a ceremony, he took the occasion to publicly chastise the president for going to Germany. Nancy was stunned by Wiesel's words and became even more angry about the mess "I'd gotten them into."

I considered resigning on the spot, as if that would help, and approached Nancy with the idea.

"Nonsense," she responded, unwilling even to consider my offer, but that didn't soften her attitude toward me.

In the past, whenever we had been at odds, it was over whether we should do something and how it ought to be handled; always, we both knew that we ultimately had the president's good in mind. Now, Nancy was convinced I had perhaps ruined her husband's presidency, and maybe the rest of his life in the bargain. It felt like a stab to the heart. I had spent a dozen years protecting him and his image. The last thing I wanted to be remembered for was ruining his legacy. It was by far the worst public relations crisis that had happened to Reagan since he was elected, and it was my fault.

My last conversation with Nancy about Bitburg was a late-afternoon phone call. She rang me in my office from the residence, and we had a very painful, very emotional confrontation. I was already a wreck because I had let Ronald Reagan down. Disappointing Nancy like this compounded the problem tenfold.

Finally, I realized our conversation was going nowhere; so I let her finish her verbal tirade, then said, "Nancy, it's done. If going into a panic would help, then I'd panic, but I am trying my damnedest to make it right. Let me get on with it, **please.**"

I hung up, and we didn't speak again for some time. I know Nancy had an equally difficult talk with the president not long after she talked with me, but she didn't make any more headway than I did against him. "The final word has been spoken as far as I'm concerned," the president said afterward, and that was it.

I did have one last trick up my sleeve: against my earlier instincts, I had talked the president into visiting the concentration camp at Bergen Belsen, prior to laying the wreath at Bitburg, and I had lined up a rabbi to stand beside him as he toured the camp. The image of reconciliation, I hoped, might at least partially counter the later ones from Bitburg that were sure to show the "SS Waffen" gravestones. But even that idea would come to nothing.

The president's plane was on the way from Bonn to Bitburg, by way of Bergen-Belsen, when I knocked on the door of the Reagans' cabin. It was early in the morning and I had to tell him that the rabbi had called in the middle of the night to cancel. He was feeling too much heat. Nancy didn't look up as I entered. Her face seemed ashen. When she finally did fix me with a glance, her expression spoke volumes: why had I stuck another knife in their backs?

That afternoon, Reagan stood with Helmut Kohl at Bitburg, laid the wreath as planned, and spoke the words that were in his heart to say:

> We are here because humanity refuses to accept that freedom or the spirit of man can ever be extinguished. We are here to commemorate that life triumphed over tragedy and the death of the Holocaust— overcame the suffering, the sickness, the testing, and, yes, the gassings. . . . Out of the ashes, hope; and from the pain, promise.

Nancy got through that day, as she got through many other trying ones, and she and Reagan patched up their differences over Bitburg in short order. Even their worst fights weren't very dramatic. They simply got quiet with each other. The madder they were, the more silence there was between them: you could measure the rift with almost scientific precision once you got used to the warning signs, but you had to act quickly because they could never stay angry at each other for very long. Nancy says that years ago while on vacation with her parents, her mother described a chat she overheard newlyweds having at poolside. The bride was teary-eyed, and her husband asked what was the matter. "You were cool to me in the pool," was the bride's response. For some reason, that little phrase stuck with Nancy, and whenever a rare rift occurred between them, either Reagan or Nancy would use that little phrase to put things right again.

Nancy and I eventually patched things up, too, both feeling a little foolish for doubting Ronald Reagan's strength and vision. And this time, at least, it wasn't Nancy who had taken the whipping in the media.

Even during the tough times, I could clearly see what motivated Nancy Reagan. Simply put, she has a big heart. If you're lucky enough to be her friend, you have a devoted, lifetime pal. And it doesn't matter who you are, what your station in life is, or where you come from. Take a peek at her Christmas list. Sure, it has the rich and famous of the world—artists, actors, and entrepreneurs, and plenty of politicians and other movers and shakers. But it is equally weighted toward folks you may not expect to be there at all: barbers, pharmacists, cleaners, and the like. And she would help each and every one of them.

I remember getting a late-night phone call after one of Nancy's closest pals, Truman Capote, was tossed into a Southern California jail for disorderly conduct. I was laughing under my breath, wondering exactly what indecencies the author of **In Cold Blood** might have committed. But Nancy was convinced the frail, effeminate Capote wouldn't survive in confinement. Since Nancy viewed me as a troubleshooter, she called me at home, begging me to get him out of the slammer.

"I'm not a lawyer," I protested. "What can I do?"

"I don't know, but what I do know is that jail will kill him," she said. Her voice was trembling.

I called Mr. Dependable, Ed Meese, another longtime Reagan man and an attorney, who sprang into action and saw that Capote was released immediately.

Of course, Capote, who died in 1997, was a celebrity, but that wasn't the point. The point is that he was her friend, and even if he hadn't had two dimes to rub together, she would have treated him the same way. That's the great heart that the press and general public so rarely got to see, but plenty of people got to see it in private—from Truman Capote to the Texas mother with the addict son to all those sick and wounded and elderly people that Nancy used to win over in an instant during her hospital visits.

Armed with nothing but a warm smile and a tough disposition, Nancy met with the families of the victims of the 1983 Soviet attack on a Korean airliner and took every one of them into her arms. Given her nature and her heart, she couldn't have done anything else. That same scene repeated itself at Camp Lejeune later that year, after the bombing of the U.S. Marine barracks in Beirut. The first lady spent hours comforting the families of the dead. Yes, Ronald Reagan was along on both occasions. He was the star attraction, as always. But it's Nancy those of us who were there remember, not her husband-president. Ronald Reagan tended to respond in kind: if you reached out to him, he would reach out to you. I know it's not her image, but Nancy naturally reached out to people and pulled them into her, transferring strength.

Warmth doesn't always do the trick. Sometimes it takes good old-fashioned flirting to get what you want, and believe me, Nancy is no slouch at that either. When she has to, she can charm the last dollar out of your wallet. They say that Helen of Troy's face launched a thousand ships. Well, Nancy's flirting, I contend, helped to end the cold war as we knew it for more than four decades.

When Reagan first came into office, he made no bones about being sick and tired of containing the Soviets. Maybe, he said, it was time to start "rolling them back." For this, he was relentlessly assaulted by liberals and pacifists for being an unrepentant warmonger, a cowboy, a baby killer—take your pick. To Nancy, these attacks were as painful as they were vexing: hadn't the voters sent Jimmy Carter back to Georgia precisely because of his weak foreign policy?

Nancy also knew that the real reason her husband had run for president in the first place was that he felt destined to try to end the cold war and snuff out the threat of a nuclear apocalypse. In his homespun way, Reagan was convinced he could move peace forward if only he could form a personal bond with his Soviet counterpart, but Moscow's leaders kept dying on him, and bureaucrats on both sides of the great ideological divide always got in the way.

To break the logjam, Nancy sought out George Shultz and let him know that Ronald Reagan wanted to act, and act decisively, in his dealings with the Soviets. Working with her, I arranged at the president's direction for Shultz and national security adviser Bill Clark to meet weekly in private session with the president to formulate a new approach, one that would open a fresh channel to the Soviet leadership and take the level of contact to a different level, bypassing the imagination-challenged bureaucrats of both superpowers.

As a critical part of that effort, Reagan was meeting in the Oval Office with the Soviet ambassador to the United States, Andrei Gromyko, one day around noon when Nancy slipped in from the Red Room and began her own personal détente charm blitz. Over drinks—Perrier for Nancy, fruit juice for the Russian—the two exchanged small talk until Gromyko finally leaned toward the first lady and asked:

"Does your husband believe in peace or war?"

"Peace," Nancy assured him.

"You're sure?"

She said she was, and the conversation went back to smaller subjects, but as it came time for the two men to head in to a working lunch together, Gromyko again leaned toward Nancy, this time counseling her: "Whisper the word **peace** to your husband every night."

Nancy took the ambassador by the hand, gave him her most flirtatious and unforgettable smile, and said, "I will, and I'll also whisper it in your ear."

To me, the moment is an almost perfect metaphor for Nancy's entire role in the Reagan White House: quiet, subtle, and direct. Maybe it wasn't a critical difference, but as Joe Califano pointed out: sometimes in the most complex situations, the simplest approaches work best.

Of all the challenges posed by life in that madhouse at 1600 Pennsylvania Avenue, the greatest might come when the principals themselves fall ill. Then, everything gets magnified to the nth degree: the concern, the attention, the coverage, the consequences. There's no good way to come down with cancer anywhere, but to come down with it when your address is the White House, Washington, D.C., can ratchet everything up to the breaking point. I'm still astounded that the Reagans survived the experience—twice.

For Nancy, I'm sure, Reagan's colon cancer was by far the greater concern. He was, after all, the president, and the 1985 surgery to excise the tumor was serious enough that the powers of his office were transferred to Vice President Bush for about eight hours. But it wasn't just the disease that worried Nancy. She also had Reagan's retinue of advisers to deal with, most notably Don Regan.

Regan had taken over as chief of staff at the start of the second term. A marine colonel in the Pacific during World War II and the former head

of Merrill Lynch, he was used to having people
jump when he barked, whoever they were. The
president was no sooner out of the hospital and
sitting up in his White House bed then Regan
began to insist that he get back to work. People
need to see that you're in charge, he kept telling
the boss, and they won't believe it until you're
sitting in the Oval Office. Left to his own devices, Reagan probably would have pulled on his
blue suit and set off downstairs to work, but
Nancy would have none of it. The more Regan
insisted, the more the mother hen took over. By
the end, she all but posted a guard at her husband's bedroom door to make sure he couldn't
get out, and his chief of staff couldn't get in.

Nancy's own breast cancer was diagnosed two
years later. Both Reagans had had annual physicals for as long as I can remember, and Nancy always had a yearly mammogram. By early in the
second term, the White House physician was John
Hutton, a military doctor assigned by the army.
Nancy was attracted by Hutton's gentlemanly
manner; she also liked and trusted him because he
was congenitally incapable of sugarcoating bad
news. Still, Nancy told me, she found it odd when
Hutton accompanied her to the Bethesda Naval
Hospital for her regularly scheduled physical on
October 6, 1987. The White House physician
normally doesn't travel with the first lady for a
routine test. For his part, Hutton said recently

that he had no knowledge of any problem with Nancy; he just decided to go with her.

Nancy recalls feeling pretty good during that drive up to Maryland. She was in the middle of some tough times—the Iran-Contra scandal was enveloping her husband's administration—yet she says she was chipper until after the first mammogram when the nurse asked her to stay undressed so they could take another. That's when the "flags went up in my head," Nancy says. After the next procedure, Hutton came back into the room, sat down, and told Nancy in his unvarnished way that she seemed to have a "tumor in her left breast." A biopsy later, Hutton gave her a second, more imposing blow. "It's cancer."

The pair drove back to the White House in complete silence. Hutton gently escorted the first lady to the residence. On the way, they agreed that he would be the one to tell the president, who at the time was in the Oval Office. Hutton tells me that he'll never forget the look on the president's face—one of despair, but also of disbelief. "I really believe Reagan thought that nothing bad would ever happen to his Nancy," Hutton says.

I was gone from the White House by then, heading through my own personal hell: dealing with an investigation, indictment, and trial; and coming to terms with my addiction to alcohol. It was an awful time, for me and my family, but no moment was worse than when Carolyn learned, after all our other misery, that she, too, had breast cancer. Her surgery and chemotherapy, and the anxious waiting afterward, were as bad as life gets, but we at least had our privacy by then.

As first lady, Nancy didn't have the luxury of privacy, so she did the next best thing: used her diagnosis and subsequent mastectomy as a kind of national teachable moment. Just as Ron's openness about his colon cancer alerted aging baby boomers and older males to the need for colonoscopies, so Nancy's frankness about her breast cancer helped to drive up interest in self-exams and mammograms, as well as bolster general understanding of the often lethal disease. The front-line defenses against both forms of cancer were strengthened immeasurably by the Reagans' willingness to confront their own cancers publicly and head-on.

I sometimes think that the Reagans' separate and collective reactions to their cancers were among their finest hours, but then I remember that they had been in training for moments like this for half a decade. An assassin's bullets had gone a long way toward preparing them for the worst life has to offer.

4

"YOUR HUSBAND WASN'T HIT"

For a place that's at the center of so much conflict, the White House can be a deceptively peaceful place to live. The morning of the day Ronald Reagan was nearly killed by an assassin's bullet, he awakened at 7 A.M., as always, showered, dressed, and joined Nancy for breakfast, either a bowl of cereal or an egg. Reagan was disciplined in all things, eating included. When he left the second-floor residence, he and Nancy embraced and kissed as if he were going away to war or a three-month safari, instead of a few steps to the Oval Office in the West Wing. The usual round of meetings waited, but it was not an arduous day. The speech he was giving early that afternoon at the Washington Hilton hotel was a little inside-the-Beltway affair, to a bunch of tough union guys who were sure to be eating out of his hand by the end.

After sending her husband off to the Oval Office, Nancy skimmed the morning's papers, then dressed, probably silently counting her blessings. On this particular day in late March, Nancy had left a luncheon at the Phillips Gallery early because, as she explained to me later, "I had this premonition. I was overcome with the feeling that something was terribly wrong, and I never had this feeling before. All I knew was that I had to get back to the White House." When she returned and found everything seeming alright, she continued her schedule and began an informal meeting in the third-floor solarium with the chief usher and a decorator. The chief usher is the majordomo of the White House, in charge of all services from cooks and launderers to the maintenance staff. Nancy had brought the decorator in to help rescue the executive mansion from Jimmy and Rosalynn Carter's southern motif. Nancy had a vision of California on the Potomac, and she was itching to get started on it. Tara North wasn't quite her style.

Nancy was in midsentence with the decorator and chief usher when her lead Secret Service agent, George Opfer, interrupted her.

"There's been a shooting at the hotel," he said. "Your husband wasn't hit."

Opfer told her that the president's limousine had been diverted to the George Washington University Hospital as a precaution. Others in the presidential party hadn't fared so well. The agent didn't have the names yet or the details, but several people had been hit. It was one of those moments, Nancy told me later, when relief and horror mixed in equal measure.

At just about the same moment, I was placing a call from the hospital to the White House in hopes of briefing Jim Baker and Ed Meese. Both, I knew, would be anxious to get to the president's side, but I begged them first to convince Nancy not to come. It might sound cold now, but even though I had seen others shot and the president take a nasty stumble, I didn't think he was in any real danger. I also truly—and wrongly—believed that Nancy's arrival would only complicate matters. Forgetting she knew her way around a hospital, I worried that the sight of blood, even if it wasn't her husband's, would shake her up.

In fact, I was already too late. If Reagan was at the George Washington University Hospital, Nancy was going to be there with him, come hell or high water. Even if he wasn't seriously hurt, others would need comforting. When her Secret Service detail urged her to stay where she was, Nancy simply announced that she would walk the dozen or so blocks to the hospital if the Secret Service wouldn't drive her. Knowing she was serious, her lead agent gave the high sign, and a car pulled up to the East Wing within seconds.

Twenty minutes earlier, with the smell of

cordite still hanging in the air, her husband had been whisked away from the Washington Hilton in a small, silent convoy: no sirens, no blaring lights, just two limousines. Ronald Reagan and Secret Service agent Jerry Parr sat in the back of the first; I followed in the trailing car. Behind us, Press Secretary Jim Brady, D.C. policeman Thomas Delahanty, and Secret Service agent Tim McCarthy lay sprawled on the sidewalk next to the hotel, brought down by John Hinckley Jr.'s bullets. Our two cars maintained radio silence as we went. No one knew if Hinckley had acted alone or was part of some larger plot to decapitate the government. I had been surprised, then, when the lead limo veered off Connecticut Avenue. Only later would I learn that as the president was laying into Jerry Parr for tackling him too hard back at the hotel and cramming him into the car, Jerry noticed a pink froth around Reagan's lips. A broken rib, maybe, and a punctured lung, Jerry surmised. There was still no thought that the president had been shot, but Jerry redirected the limo to the hospital. In that moment, I'm convinced, he saved Ronald Reagan's life.

Now, Nancy Reagan, too, was making the trip to the hospital without benefit of a lead car or motorcycle escort to pave the way. All the normal protocols of presidential travel in the nation's capital had been turned on their head. The first lady would have to sit in traffic like everyone else. Just as Nancy was contemplating a run for it, the gridlock broke and her car shot forward. I can only imagine what the agents in that car were going through, trying to keep her calm as they crept along Pennsylvania Avenue, not knowing what awaited them.

At the hospital, the Secret Service let me know that Nancy Reagan was approaching, and I went out to meet her. By 1981, I had known Nancy for almost fifteen years. She and Reagan were more to me than just my bosses: the affection I have for both of them transcends words. I was glad I was the first person Nancy saw at the hospital that fateful afternoon, but I also knew I would have to tell her what she didn't want to hear. In the short time between my call to the White House and Nancy's arrival, I had been in to see the president. I knew now that he hadn't just been roughed up by an admirably aggressive Secret Service agent.

I'll never forget what I saw when I stepped into the room where Reagan was being frantically worked on. My friend, my president, was stripped naked. One of the doctors was holding his suit jacket up to the light. The doc and his team were examining a tiny hole under the left sleeve, but I couldn't take my eyes off Reagan. He had lost all color—as gray as you can be and still be alive, I thought. His eyes were wide open and very moist. He was staring blankly at the ceiling. I had to lean on the doorjamb for support; otherwise, I might have passed out. I remember thinking at that moment: I don't want Nancy to see this. Nancy Reagan is strong, but seeing her Ronnie like this could break her.

It had been only a few hours since I had last seen the first lady, but it felt like a month. Where to start? I tried to collect my thoughts, put them in some kind of cohesive order for the flood of questions I'd be fielding from her and from others that day—and for the rest of my life, as events turned out. I'd watched Reagan finish his speech at the Hilton with his usual flair, then grip and grin with the adoring audience. I was by the president's side as he headed for the limo and directly in front of him when John Hinckley emptied his chamber and four good men hit the ground. To this day, I don't know how he missed me. I was surrounded by the guys who got shot.

All of it—the sound of the gunshots, the smell of the cordite, the silent race back down Connecticut Avenue, the ashen president I had just seen—was on my mind as Nancy's car raced into the main entrance of the hospital and I walked briskly to greet her.

Nancy jumped out of the car before it even

came to a complete stop. As usual, I didn't beat around the bush with her.

"He's been hit," I said.

"But they told me he wasn't hit," she managed to reply.

When I didn't answer, her voice became sterner: "I've got to see him."

Secret Service and other security personnel, media, doctors, nurses, and orderlies were buzzing all around us, but nobody seemed to notice Nancy and me having our heart-to-heart. It was surreal, a barely controlled chaos, like five one-act plays being performed on one stage at the same time.

"They told me he wasn't hit," she said again.

"Well, he was," I said limply. "The docs tell me it's not that serious."

Even today, that sounds ludicrous. First, nobody told me that. Second, how can it not be "serious" when a seventy-year-old takes a bullet from point-blank range? I was grasping at straws, trying to delude myself as much as Nancy, I suppose, but all I succeeded in doing was making her more agitated.

"Where? Where was he hit?" she demanded.

"They don't know yet. I think they're still looking for the bullet," I explained.

This didn't go over well at all.

"You don't understand, I have to see him, and

he has to see me. That's the way it is," she said. "Please, Mike, tell them I have to see him."

I consulted briefly with Daniel Ruge, the president's physician, then escorted Nancy into a small office that had been made available to us and left her there while I went to check on the status of the president. She didn't have to sit alone for long. Paul Laxalt, the Nevada senator and one of Reagan's closest friends, had already made it to the hospital; he began to comfort Nancy in that tiny office. John Simpson, the head of the Secret Service and another close Reagan friend, joined them.

Whatever their private reservations, the doctors in charge of the president's care gave me the okay to bring Nancy into the examining room, so I retrieved her from the office, then stood off in the corner and watched as she approached her suddenly gaunt and gray husband. Reagan was still in the same position I had seen him in earlier, only this time he was wearing an oxygen mask. His lips were caked with dried blood. The blank stare, at least, was gone. The president knew where he was and why. His first words to his wife went to the core of what kind of man he is.

"Honey," he somehow whispered around the mask, "I forgot to duck."

Minutes later, I took the shaken first lady by the arm and escorted her out of her husband's room. I wanted to try to comfort her in any way possible, but she spoke before I could think what to say: "Oh, Mike, he's so pale."

"I know," I told her, "but if you think he's bad now, you should have been here an hour ago."

Nancy paused and looked at me with an expressionless face. My words weren't very comforting, but she understood my meaning.

Soon, word came down to us that Reagan was losing too much blood. The surgeons needed to operate immediately. As they wheeled the president toward the operating room, Nancy walked with him, holding his hand as tightly as she could.

While we awaited word from the surgeons, Nancy and I sat in a private room, watching television in silence. We were getting most of our information live from our old friend, ABC anchor Frank Reynolds. Nancy and I watched Reynolds as he told the nation, erroneously, that Jim Brady had died, only to retract the news shortly thereafter. Reynolds immediately apologized, while at the same time exploding with rage, telling his crew live on the air that they damn well better do a better job of fact-checking. I'd seen Jim wheeled into the hospital, flat on his back, looking lifeless, and could understand how Reynolds's people got it wrong. We switched briefly to another network only to hear that Reagan was getting prepped for open-heart surgery—another error. Nancy gasped but otherwise stared at the screen stoically.

We then watched Secretary of State Al Haig announce in a shaking voice in the White House press room—in front of a huge, shaken national TV audience—that "he was now in charge at the White House." Nancy and I looked at each other in utter shock as Haig made the pronouncement. As Frank Reynolds quickly pointed out, the secretary of state would have to get in line. The constitutionally mandated order of succession runs from the vice president, to the Speaker of the House and president pro tem of the Senate before it gets to cabinet members. It would have taken a massive conspiracy before Al would have been sitting in the Oval Office. And, of course, Vice President Bush was alive and well on an air force plane heading back toward Washington.

I've always thought that what Al was trying to say was not that he was now the president, but that someone was in charge. After sprinting up the stairs from the situation room to the press room, he would have done well to rest a moment and catch his breath. He would have sounded more in charge if he hadn't been almost gasping and sweating on the brow.

When Nancy finally tired of watching the drama unfold on the television, I suggested we go to the small hospital chapel to pray. There, Nancy and I were joined by George Opher and

Sarah Brady, Jim's wife. It was the first time I had ever met Sarah Brady. I know it was Nancy's first time, too. The two women embraced without speaking. Sarah was holding up remarkably well. Tim McCarthy's parents were also in the chapel, and Nancy embraced them and told them how grateful she was for their son's heroism and dedication. She was praying for him, too, she told them. Sarah left the chapel first, to go see what she could learn about Jim. The McCarthys were still there when Nancy and I took our leave.

Back in our makeshift office, Nancy pressed the medical staff for more information. The nurses were surprisingly forthcoming, providing far more frequent updates than I had anticipated. One nurse told us that the doctors were close to sewing up the president without finding the elusive bullet. Neither Nancy nor I knew that bullets are frequently left in bodies with few repercussions. Not long afterward, another nurse came by with a clarification: they had found the bullet. But she had a frightening tale about the path it had traveled.

The president, she told us, had not been hit directly. Rather the damage had been done by a fragment of a bullet that had split apart as it ricocheted off the armored car of his limousine. The fragment pierced him below the armpit—he had his arm raised in a typical Reagan wave as

Hinckley fired—traversed several inches down his left side, where it bounced off an unsuspecting rib, punctured his lung, and then completed its destructive journey about an inch from Ronald Reagan's heart.

Nancy was just absorbing how close her husband had come to being killed on the spot when Ron Jr. and his wife, Doria, came racing into the hospital. As soon as he heard about the shooting, Ron had chartered a private plane to get to Washington from the Midwest. The other Reagan children, we learned, would be arriving the next morning. Ron gave his mother another, invaluable shoulder to lean on.

We eventually talked Nancy into returning to the White House that evening. The public's worry couldn't crest, we argued, so long as the first lady remained at the hospital. There would always be the suspicion that the public wasn't being told the full story. By leaving her husband alone, Nancy would signal the country—and the world—that the Gipper would soon be back in the saddle. With enormous reluctance, she finally agreed.

Ron Jr. had preceded us and was waiting at the White House, along with George Bush, when we arrived later that evening. Fatigued and shaken, Nancy embraced them both, then headed to her private quarters. She would later tell me that night in the White House was the loneliest night she had ever spent. Her diary entry reflects as much, saying in characteristically direct language that if Reagan did not make it, her "life would be over."

By the next morning, Ronald Reagan wanted answers. Although he was still in serious condition and now completely unable to speak because of the tube down his throat, the Great Communicator had a notepad at hand, and he was making full use of it.

Reagan's first note expressed his hunch that others had fallen that day. The news of Brady's paralysis and the others brought him to tears. Almost immediately, he directed Jim Baker and me to make sure that his stricken press secretary retain his title until the president's term ended. That symbolic but warm gesture allowed Brady to keep the job and the pay for the next seven years.

Not surprisingly to me, Reagan asked next about the shooter, whose name he still didn't know.

"What happened to the guy with the gun? What was his beef?"

The wording of that question, and the view of life it rested upon, says volumes about the dramatic difference between Ronald and Nancy Reagan. Although he was the one who had been grievously wounded, the president's first instinct was to forgive. Shortly after he got his voice back, Reagan told me, "I began to pray for the men shot, but I realized that if I was going to do what was right, I'd have to pray for that boy who shot us, too."

Nancy would have none of that.

On the day of the shooting, the Reagans received a telegram from John Hinckley's mortified parents. Their words were poignant, yet terse: "Words cannot express our sorrow over the tragic events of today. We are praying that God will comfort you with His love, grace, and peace."

Nancy told me she felt for the parents, but she simply could not find room in her heart to forgive Hinckley. While Reagan prayed for his would-be assassin, Nancy began pressuring the Secret Service to do more to protect the president. Later, she would lean on me to develop new ways to keep her husband away from large gaggles of reporters, the kind Hinckley had hidden among. To this day, Nancy worries that somehow John Hinckley will be released from St. Elizabeth's, the D.C. psychiatric hospital where he has been confined for more than twenty years, and try again to harm her husband.

The rest of the Reagan family sided with Nancy, seething with contempt toward Hinckley. Nancy remembers Patti especially boiling over when discussing the gunman who had nearly murdered her father. Dad refused to join in.

"You know, Patti," he told her, "when I was lying there in the hospital wondering if I was going to die, I spent a lot of time praying, and I knew I couldn't just pray for myself. I had to pray for John Hinckley, too. If God loves me, then in spite of everything, He must also love John Hinckley."

The doctors predicted the president would need at least two weeks in the hospital to recover from his wounds sufficiently to return to the White House. Dismissing them with a wave of his hand, the president informed the medical staff, Nancy, me, and everyone else in attendance that he was a fast healer and to call for the limo. Nancy and the docs won that battle, but even though he had to remain in the hospital, the Gipper was irrepressible.

Eventually, the stories would become the stuff of modern legend, a chronicle of casual courage, much of it expressed—at least early on—on the notepads the president kept by his side while the tube was still in his throat. Nancy found some of the notes inspiring; others had a gallows humor to them. But serious or not, they clearly demonstrated—to me anyway—the toughness of the man.

"I'm still alive, aren't I?" was one of his earliest offerings.

"All in all, I'd rather be in Philadelphia," he wrote on another occasion, stealing a classic from W. C. Fields.

Then, in an ode to Churchill, "There is no more exhilarating feeling than being shot at without result."

The Hollywood Reagan revealed himself on paper as well. "Can we rewrite this scene beginning at the time I left the hotel?" And "Send me back to L.A. where I can see the air I'm breathing."

To the nurse who combed his hair and mischievously, but too obviously, checked out the presidential mane for lurking grays: "Now you can tell the world that I don't dye my hair!"

Maybe the best story of them all comes from George Bush. When the vice president walked into Reagan's hospital room, he was aghast to see his boss on his hands and knees in the bathroom, wiping up spilled water. Forbidden to shower because of a fever and feeling gritty, Reagan had decided to give himself a sponge bath.

Easing up to his side, the vice president gently admonished the Leader of the Free World: "You should let the nurse clean that up."

"Oh no," the president replied. "I'm the guy who disobeyed orders. If the doctors see the nurse mopping it up, she'll get in trouble."

Clearly this was a man determined to be sprung from his hospital cell, no matter how close a bullet had come to his heart. I remember walking out behind the first couple when the president was finally set free and noticing many of the medical staff holding back tears. Mindful of what had brought him to the hospital in the first place, the president had donned a sweater that concealed a bulletproof vest.

It was a rainy day, and I hopped into a car with Dan Ruge, who would be spending the next few nights in the Lincoln Bedroom, just in case. The two weeks had taken a toll on everybody, and the president's physician was no exception. I looked over to him to ask him a question and noticed tears welling in his reddened eyes. "You know, Mike, we could have easily been leaving here in a very different way." All I could do was nod in agreement.

As Ruge and I pulled up behind the Reagans on the return to 1600 Pennsylvania Avenue, I was overwhelmed by the reception of the White House staff. Reagan relished the homecoming, too. Acknowledging the staff upon his triumphant entrance, he instinctively raised his left hand in an easy wave—the same one I had last seen a few weeks ago at the Hilton Hotel. I winced at the irony, but I doubt if the president thought about it for a moment. To his mind, the shooting was old news. Time to move on. Besides, there were better images to soak in. A stunning rainbow had arched over the executive mansion, perhaps a welcome-home gift from God himself. I wondered at the time if anyone else made the connection between this heavenly sight and Nancy's Secret Service code name: Rainbow.

Inside, Nancy had filled the residence with flowers. Chocolate chip cookies, Reagan's favorite, were never more than a short reach away. She made sure, too, that the kitchen was stocked with macaroni and cheese and other presidential favorites. To the untrained eye, Nancy was just glad to have Reagan safe by her side again, but those of us who knew her better could see that Nancy was very wired, very uptight. Even Reagan's short walk from the hospital entrance to the waiting limo had unnerved her. Months would pass before she could begin to relax when the president was out in public for even a few minutes.

In the aftermath of her husband's near-death experience, Nancy began to take stock of her own life—what she had and what she had almost lost. By way of expressing her gratitude toward the medical staff at George Washington University Hospital, she began inviting some of Reagan's doctors to coveted state dinners. Officer Delahanty, Secret Service agent McCarthy, and of course Jim Brady were never far from her mind either. I'm sure that even now she measures their suffering against her own.

Nancy remained serious, too, about doing something to make sure that this would not happen again. John Hinckley Jr. might have been a deranged, solo gunman, but six of the shots he fired at a presidential party protected by the Secret Service had found human targets. Ronald Reagan had been in office less than three months, but Nancy began sifting through all the details of those days, asking herself if there was anything she could have done to head off the assassination attempt. In fact, such a fear had been with her long before March 30, 1981.

Ronald Reagan once called 1600 Pennsylvania an "eight-star hotel," fully equipped with an army of butlers and maids and cooks who at a moment's notice would rustle up the finest meals, build roaring fires, and even make sure every clock was on time to the second. It was a gilded life, and Nancy Reagan was grateful for it and not immune to its charms. But through all the years of campaigning for governor, the eight years in Sacramento, and stumping for president in 1968, 1976, and 1980, Nancy constantly worried about Reagan's safety.

She had visions of Jack Kennedy, George Wallace, and Martin Luther King, Jr. Bobby Kennedy's June 1968 assassination in Los Angeles brought the danger home to California and served as a tragic, pointed reminder of the risks of pursuing elective office. At the time of the murder, Governor Reagan was being pressured to mount a last-minute opposition to Richard Nixon for the Republican presidential nomination. The Secret Service provided him with his own security detail, and it wasn't long before the detail proved its worth. Nancy relayed the story to me the following morning.

One night in that tempestuous summer of 1968, the Reagans were awoken in the middle of the night by a gunshot. Reagan dashed out of the bedroom to find a Secret Service agent racing up the stairs, rifle at the ready. "Would you mind not getting in front of any windows?" he ordered the governor and his wife. Turns out, one of the agents assigned to the Reagans had spotted two men lighting a Molotov cocktail in the yard, directly below their bedroom windows. The agent fired instantly on the intruders but missed, and the would-be assassins got away, leaving behind a store of gasoline-filled bottles—large ones, topped to the brim. Almost certainly, the Reagans would have burned to death if not for the Secret Service.

On another occasion back in the Sacramento days, Nancy learned of a threat we were trying to keep secret from her: a plan to kidnap her in an effort to force her husband-governor to release certain prisoners from the California penal system. If Reagan refused, the kidnappers were going to send him Nancy's severed head in a box. Undercover sources tipped police to the plot before it got off the ground, but the gruesomeness of it lingered long in her thoughts.

As Reagan convalesced from the March 30, 1981, assassination attempt, he didn't appear to be bothered in the least by the threat of other, new attempts on his life. Far from it, in fact. I was with Reagan nearly every day after the attempt on his life and saw close up how his brush with death changed him. The bullet, in my view, had a liberating effect on the man. It freed him to become even more reliant on his own instincts. He started listening less to his counselors and more to his core beliefs. This feeling of being "spared"—as he called it—allowed him to approach the Soviets in a way that **he,** not State Department diplomats, believed was right. The country—and the world—is a better, safer place today for that.

Although she tried to hide it from her husband, Nancy changed, too. She lost weight and couldn't sleep. She prayed incessantly and cried alone. I never saw Nancy as a superstitious person, but after the assassination attempt, she became consumed with her husband's safety. Like any spouse whose mate had just been shot, Nancy worried about everything. Unlike other spouses, though, she was married to the president of the United States at a time in history when someone seemed to have declared open season on American and global leaders. Not long after Ronald Reagan was fired on at point-blank range, Pope John Paul II was shot and Egypt's Anwar el-Sadat murdered.

During our recent conversations about the attempt on her husband's life, Nancy reminded me about the "twenty-year thing," as she called it. For more than a hundred years, every president elected in a "zero" year—as Reagan had been in 1980, and Abraham Lincoln in 1860—died in office. This didn't help. Nor did the media help by chewing endlessly on the ghoulish coincidence. Nancy also worried that Ronald Reagan's remarkable resilience would challenge other John Hinckleys to finish his work.

Ironically, as Reagan recovered, Nancy became more and more troubled, turning to ministers, friends, and family for answers, support, and ideas. Before long, she was seeking help from a highly unusual source.

One of the people Nancy leaned on most was television talk-show host and producer Merv Griffin, a longtime friend. Merv reminded Nancy that he had introduced her to astrologer Joan Quigley in the late 1970s, after Joan had done a guest turn on **The Merv Griffin Show**. The most stunning news Merv had for Nancy was that Joan said that she had known in advance that something bad was going to happen to the president on March 30, 1981. A chill ran down

Nancy's spine: My God, she thought, I could have prevented this.

Nancy immediately called Joan to get her side of the story. Yes, the Californian astrologer confirmed, she had seen in advance that March 30 was going to be a bad day for Ronald Reagan. The more Nancy dwelled on what Joan had told her, the more she became convinced it would be a good idea to run dates and times past Quigley in hopes of seeing if simple schedule changes might prevent another attempt on Reagan's life. When I look back, perhaps I should have tried harder to veto the whole business, but who was I to tell her it was a bad idea when she was convinced the well-being of her husband was at stake?

I don't believe that we can see the future in the stars, but if Nancy did and if taking note of the stars made her feel better, that was good enough for me. While Joan was a minor inconvenience to me, I could see how important this was to the first lady. Nancy was the strategist of the first couple, the worrier, the one who could never just sit back and let fate happen the way her husband could. She needed to be in action, and an astrological consultation every few weeks seemed to me then—and still does—an innocent enough quirk.

Nancy would talk with Joan a couple of times

a month, schedule in hand, then report back to me if there was a "bad day" looming on the president's calendar. Sometimes I'd make the recommended scheduling change. More often, I was very frank in telling the first lady that an event or a trip simply could not be moved, and that would be the end of it. The consultations were never a burden—far from it, they were a comfort to Nancy during a very hard time. Contrary to press reports, the astrologer had no impact on Reagan's policies or his politics. Nada. Zero. Zilch.

Reagan himself didn't know anything about Nancy's astrologer until he overheard her in the residence talking on the phone with Quigley. I felt under no obligation to tell him; indeed, I felt as though I would have been violating a trust if I had. But once the secret was out within the family, all three of us agreed on the need to keep this quiet. Nancy had been beaten up enough in the media. Word that she was in league with some star charter would be like tossing raw steak to a pack of hungry wolves.

That the Joan Quigley story wasn't kept quiet, that it did leak out, that the media ended up having (just as predicted) a raucous field day with it all, is at least partially my fault. "Astrologer Runs White House" was only one of many memorable headlines. Ouch. Here's how it happened.

• • •

During one of my last days in the White House in 1985, incoming chief of staff Donald Regan asked me to sit down for a debriefing. He wanted to get my advice on White House management. Since I had then been with the Reagans for almost two decades, he was looking especially for insight into how to deal with the first couple. As we were wrapping up our meeting, I paused to think if I had missed anything that Don should know about.

"There is one more little thing," I remember saying. "Ever since Reagan was shot, Nancy's been consulting an astrologer to make sure it doesn't happen again. Thought you should know, just in case."

If Regan cared, he didn't show it. He brushed the comment aside as if I had told him it was going to rain next Tuesday. "Is that right?" I think he said. Certainly not much more.

A few days later, I left the White House for good, Don Regan took over control of the president's schedule, and a new era in the Ronald Reagan administration got under way. By then, many of the vast improvements in presidential security that Nancy had been pushing for since the 1981 shooting had been put into effect. The president was, in fact, safer almost everywhere he went.

Nancy, I'm sure, was a little more cautious in her dealings with Regan—they had no history between them as she and I did. While Nancy continued to point out the "good days and bad days" on Reagan's schedule, she never told Don where she was getting her information. (I, of course, had already let that large cat out of the bag.) For his part, Don seems to have found Nancy's input an unneeded irritation. As noted earlier, Don was from the tough-guy mold. Catering to worried wives, even worried first ladies, wasn't high on his priority list.

Inevitably, the astrological consultations faded even further from the scheduling picture, and there the matter might have ended entirely—a tiny, tiny footnote in the long history of the Reagan years—if it hadn't been for the Iran-Contra scandal. But alas, Iran-Contra did happen, and Don Regan was forced to resign as chief of staff in its aftermath. Blaming Nancy at least in part for his dismissal, Don couldn't wait to write about Joan Quigley in his memoir, and thus even as the Iron Curtain was disappearing before our eyes, Ronald Reagan—the chief architect of that miracle—found himself answering questions about whether an astrologer was his secret secretary of state. It should be funny, but it certainly wasn't.

By telling the world what I had told him in private, Don Regan proved an old axiom of life in the nation's capital. In Washington maybe more so than any other place in America, revenge is a dish best served cold. I used to worry, I confess, that Don had done more than that: in getting back at Nancy, I feared, he had managed to tar both her and her husband's legacy for generations to come. That, at least, I don't fret about anymore. I think anyone who thinks clearly about the astrologer flap will realize now that all the tabloid headlines are ancient history, that this was a simple case of a wife watching out for the husband she loves. As for generations to come, Nancy and Ronald Reagan's legacy, separately and together, seems to grow stronger day by day.

5
LEGACY

For most first ladies, the departure from public life is less than dramatic. They grow grayer—or not, depending on their hairdressers. The years pass. Grandchildren and great-grandchildren come along. Often, their husbands predecease them, and with that the media begins to leave them alone. When their own deaths come, many newspaper readers are surprised to learn they were still alive.

A very few first ladies stay at the forefront of issues and events. Betty Ford launched her famous clinic after her own battle with addiction. Lady Bird Johnson had extensive family business interests to look after. Jackie Kennedy protected—some say created—her assassinated husband's legacy even as she was marrying Aristotle Onassis and joining the international jet set. Always outspoken as first lady, Eleanor Roosevelt continued her role as public advocate until her own death in 1962, more than a decade and a half after FDR died in office. For the worst of reasons, an unhinged and desperately melancholic Mary Todd Lincoln remained a subject of national fascination for years following her husband's assassination.

Nancy Reagan, I'm sure, would have preferred to fall into the earlier category. She never needed the media attention; indeed, for most of her public life up to that point, she had suffered from it. All Nancy ever wanted from these post–White House years was a quiet retirement, a chance to live out her years in peace with her beloved husband. That, of course, was not to be. Like Jackie Kennedy, Nancy had married not just a man, not just a president, but a symbol—as much a totem to the political right as JFK ever was to the left. Ronald Reagan brought down the Iron Curtain. He redefined public debate in America. He forced every citizen, whether they had ever voted for him or not, to confront the role of government in our everyday lives, and the limits of exactly what the federal state can do. "Revolution" is overused, to be sure, but in the phrase "Reagan Revolution" it's exactly on target. Like Jackie Kennedy, too, Nancy was not to be allowed to rest once the totem himself was gone or unable to speak for himself.

Looking back over this last decade of Nancy's life, I'm not really amazed that she carried on the fight after Alzheimer's claimed her husband's capacities. Nancy, remember, is the daughter of a single mother who went to auditions with her baby on her hip. Petite as she is and always has been, Nancy doesn't know from quit. What truly amazes me is that she has carried the torch not just in slavish devotion of Reagan, but often in anticipation of where he might be today if fate had been kinder to him. In a very real sense, I think, she is both the continuing education of a man no longer able to educate himself and the fulfillment of a woman who always had this public role in her.

Nancy didn't get to ease into her solo act in the public arena. She didn't have the luxury of letting her approach to public policy take root slowly, one complicated issue at a time. Ever since their wedding day, Nancy had been the nester, the one who took care of the family's often complicated domestic affairs. To be sure, she kept a close eye on her husband's career and on the people around him. But Nancy Reagan never dreamed that she would have to step into the political waters where her husband swam with such ease.

Alzheimer's changed that. When Ronald Reagan bowed out of public life in 1994, Nancy had no choice but to join the debate over political and social issues that, under better circumstances, she would have gladly left to her husband. In part, history had backed her into a corner. Ronald Reagan's disease made Nancy the custodian of his legacy, a legacy that millions upon millions of Americans and others around the world continue to care deeply about. And it didn't take long for the line to form at her door— a long queue of legitimate and not-so-legitimate Reaganites seeking her powerful imprimatur on various pet projects now that the Gipper could no longer give his own seal of approval.

Candidate endorsements were a natural, and Nancy got a slew of requests for them, from local offices to national ones. Wisely, she steered clear for the most part from backing specific candidates in her husband's name. That would have just eaten up her energy at a time when Reagan was beginning to need her more and more. But one request was hard to say no to.

Nancy called me in late spring of 1996 to say that Bob Dole's people had asked her to give a speech at that summer's Republican National Convention in San Diego—the first quadrennial gathering since the 1960s that wouldn't feature Ronald Reagan as a star attraction. Nancy was on edge when she phoned. She'd never done anything like this, she said. Her husband had always been the speechmaker, a role he relished. Nancy didn't even think she could attend the event without Reagan, much less address thousands of delegates and a national television audience from a cavernous hall. I told her that the party faithful would love it and that the country would welcome her with open arms. It was important for her to speak, not only for the morale of the Republican Party but also for Ron's sake. Even though he wouldn't be at the convention, he would still be able to follow her address on television. Alzheimer's hadn't yet totally incapacitated him. Seeing his beloved Nancy being cheered on by the faithful was bound to warm him.

For added incentive, there was always Bill Clinton, who had been stomping on the Reagan record at every turn. I promised to help Nancy with her remarks, and we began to work on words she would be comfortable with.

As the big day drew closer, Nancy needed considerable encouragement. Indeed, anyone who ever bought into the myth that Nancy was power-hungry or in love with the limelight had only to see her in the weeks leading up to that speech at the 1996 convention. She felt as if she had nothing of substance to offer the delegates. Nancy, I'm sure, had always understood the love that people had for Reagan, but she had misread the love people had for her, too. All she really had to do was walk out on the stage and the conventioneers would take care of the rest, I assured her, but she wasn't buying that.

To help stack the deck, I asked old friends Phil Dusenberry of BBDO and Norman Cohen to produce a video tribute to the Reagans that ran immediately before Nancy's remarks. As the lights turned back on, Nancy mysteriously appeared at the podium without a formal introduction, and the crowd stood and cheered thunderously. (Looking back, I must have had that Gridiron dinner in mind, when Nancy walked out of the rack of old clothes to the surprise and pure delight of a hard-boiled audience.) But this was different. It was pent-up emotion for the Reagan who wasn't there and deep affection for the one who was but had always stayed in the background. Now she stood alone.

Knowing Nancy, I realized she would become as emotional as the audience, but that just made the crowd cheer louder. Sometimes we humans remember only the bad things people say about us—Nancy is no different—but that night in San Diego, she got a firsthand glimpse of how people really felt about her. Yes, Reagan was the lead act, and always would be. Nancy would never confuse why she was there, why she was asked to address the convention, but by the time she was through with her remarks, she understood she had her admirers, too.

Here's what she had to say:

I want to thank you from the bottom of my heart for that film, and a special thanks for the people who were involved with putting it together. It reminded me again how grateful Ronnie and I are for the privilege that you and America gave us for the wonderful eight years in the White House.

It also reminded me of the life you gave us before that, starting with the governorship of California. A life that we never thought we'd have. It was interesting. It was challenging. It was fascinating. It was sometimes frightening. There were times when it seemed that the sun forgot to shine. But those days have dimmed in comparison to the accomplishments that now glow brightly and the remembrance of the warmth and support of so many of you across America.

Just four years ago, Ronnie stood before you and spoke for what he said might be his last speech at a Republican convention. Sadly, his words were too prophetic. When we learned of his illness, Alzheimer's, he made the decision to write his letter to the American people, and the people responded as they always do. I can't tell you what your cards and letters have meant to both of us. The love and affection from thousands of Americans has been and continues to be a strengthening force for Ronnie and me each and every day.

We have learned as too many other
families have learned of the terrible pain
and loneliness that must be endured as
each day brings another reminder of this
very long good-bye.

But Ronnie's spirit, his optimism, his
never failing belief in the strength and
goodness of America is still very strong. If
he were able to be here tonight, he would
once again remind us of the power of each
individual, urging us once again to fly as
high as our wings will take us and to never
give up on America.

I can tell you with certainty that he still
sees the shining city on the hill, a place full
of hope and promise for us all.

As you know, I am not the speechmaker
in the family, so let me close with Ronnie's
words, not mine. In that last speech four
years ago, he said, "Whatever else history
may say about me when I'm gone, I hope it
will report that I appealed to your best
hopes and not your worst fears, to your
confidence rather than your doubts, and
may all of us as Americans never forget
your heroic origins, never fail to seek divine
guidance, and never, never lose your
natural God-given optimism."

Ronnie's optimism, like America's, still

shines very brightly. May God bless him,
and from both of us, God bless America.

I was watching backstage as Nancy spoke and
could see how nervous she was despite her out-
ward calm.

"How was it?" she asked, as soon as she had
joined me. Her uncertainty stunned me.

"You were terrific," I told her. "My God, they
loved you," and indeed the response was stunning. The crowd—already on its feet—seemed to
grow in size as the applause thundered through
the hall. I hosted a party afterward, and Nancy
was glowing. So were the many old Reagan hands
who joined us. For most of us it was a first
chance to get together after the devastating news
of Ron's illness two years earlier, yet the event
was anything but glum. Nancy wasn't just her
husband's proxy; she was our animating force
that evening. As I looked around the room at the
familiar, aging faces, it was obvious that, without
ever really intending to, Nancy had taken the
legacy in hand just fine.

Later, another brick would be added to the
building of Reagan's legacy when Democrats
and Republicans alike got behind the legislation that created the Ronald Reagan Building
and International Trade Center on Fourteenth
Street in downtown Washington, D.C. The late

Democratic New York senator Daniel Patrick Moynihan—a Reagan friend and a major force in making Washington the world-class city it is today—was one of the bill's sponsors. As the building was nearing completion, a number of longtime Reagan supporters began to wonder aloud if it was right to name a sprawling federal office complex for a president who had been so stridently opposed to the many "Puzzle Palaces" that sat along the Potomac River. Surely, they argued, if the Gipper were able to chime in on his own, he would find it strange to be honored by a place meant to house as many as six thousand bureaucrats, ready to spawn innumerable intrusions into the lives and liberties of everyday Americans.

Some of the more powerful critics of the building even tried to put Nancy on the spot. For a while, rumors were flying around Capitol Hill that the Reagan Building was going to have to be dedicated without any Reagan present. But once Nancy was able to make herself heard above the din, she pooh-poohed the criticism and cheerfully announced she would attend the festivities.

Did she have reservations about the size and cost of the building? I asked her. The concrete for the building alone, I had read, was equal to over a hundred miles of two-lane highway. More than an acre of glass had been needed to cover the ten-story atrium. There were five main entrances, eighty-five elevators, eight escalators, enough monumental stairways to keep a Roman emperor purring contentedly. Wasn't this a little over the top?

"Sure," Nancy answered, "but this will be a tribute to Ronnie for generations in the nation's capital, and I'm thrilled Congress has recognized him in this way." She also pointed out to me that something like a quarter of the space was to be rented to private international trade organizations, exactly the kind of public-private cooperation that Reagan had worked so hard to foster.

Later, in her prepared remarks, Nancy astounded both me and the audience by demonstrating how thoroughly she had mastered her husband's capacity for disarming, self-deprecatory humor. Two years earlier, she had seemed almost too nervous to go onstage at the GOP convention. Now, she was right at home behind the podium. Reagan, she told listeners, had been amused to lend his name to a bar during a presidential trip to Ireland: "I'll bet you I'm the first president who ever had a pub named after him," she remembered his saying. Then she added, with a broad gesture to the vast atrium where she was speaking: "Imagine what he would think today!"

The dedication agenda was a big one, appropriate for a mammoth building that now trails only the Pentagon in size among federal facilities.

President Clinton and others joined Nancy on the podium. I had had a call earlier in the day from one of Clinton's aides, saying that the president would like fifteen minutes alone with Nancy afterward, before he returned to the White House.

"The only way that that's going to happen is if there are five television cameras and six lawyers present," I deadpanned. It was 1998. The Clinton libido had gone off the rails once again. I couldn't resist the dig, but the caller didn't appreciate the humor. The meeting, I figured, was over before it began.

Following the dedication, Nancy, my wife and I, and some other old friends convened in the holding room at the Reagan Building, enjoying some light refreshments. The presidential motorcade needed to clear out before our own two-car caravan could get Nancy back to her hotel so she could get ready for a large dinner that a group of us had planned in her honor. I can't remember what we were talking about as we waited for the high sign to head for our cars, but all of a sudden, we realized that the president of the United States was among us. Nancy had met Clinton a few times but had spent little time with him. Now, like an apparition, he had somehow slipped into the room and was enjoying a steaming cup of coffee, perfectly content it seemed to listen to us as we chatted away. A moment later, he put his cup down, took Nancy in both arms, and said, "Hillary and I pray for you every day. . . . We love you."

The response, I'm sure, is not what he had anticipated. Nancy looked as if a mugger had embraced her. She was in total shock—a look I've seen before, but not very often and never happily. Nancy was polite, but her acting skills failed to mask how clearly unsettled she was by the experience. For his part, the president seemed to sense that the lovable-rogue routine that worked with so many other ladies had no effect on Nancy Reagan. He bid a quick adieu.

The Reagan Building, of course, is only one of innumerable efforts to embed the fortieth president's name in the national memory. Another of Nancy's favorite moments in recent years was the christening in March 2001 of the navy's newest aircraft carrier, the USS **Ronald Reagan.** The evening before, old friends from California, New York, Texas, and Washington gathered in Newport News, Virginia, for a prelaunch party for Nancy—a mixture of laughter, nostalgia, and sorrow that the Gipper couldn't be on hand for what would have been one of the great moments of his life. To add to the bittersweet atmosphere, the christening coincided with the Reagans' forty-ninth wedding anniversary. The next day, amid freezing cold and an icy rain, Nancy thanked the navy for such a wonderful anniversary present and then, as President Bush stood by, cracked the ceremonial bottle of champagne on the hulking carrier.

"I wish Ronnie were here," she said, tearing up along with the rest of us, "but somehow, I think he is." Somehow, too, I think she was right.

Nancy was equally excited when Washington National Airport was rechristened Ronald Reagan Washington National Airport, but she began to have qualms when a national campaign was launched to have at least one building or facility named for the former president in each of the fifty states. Nancy appreciates the thought and the effort, but she believes—and I agree—that the impetus has to come at the local level. Any effort to strong-arm states into complying would have embarrassed the always humble Reagan, and even now, Nancy would like to protect both Reagan and his legacy from that.

"If he were able to, he'd quietly thank them but say, 'Please don't,'" she told me.

If it were up to me, there would be other, greater ceremonies for Nancy to attend, honoring her husband. I've felt for years that Ronald Reagan deserves a Nobel Peace Prize for making the world safer from communism and nuclear holocaust. That won't happen now, of course. I've long been frustrated, too, that the motion picture industry can't spare an honorary Academy Award for the Gipper. No actor has ever achieved what he did, and Nancy would be among friends when she accepted the Oscar in his name, but I suppose political sentiment is so heavily stacked against Reagan in Hollywood that this, too, will never take place.

On a few issues Nancy has simply had to intuit where her husband would be today if disease hadn't struck him down. For her, these have been the hardest moments. The world keeps changing, and if the Reagan legacy is going to have real value, it has to evolve with it. No subject has challenged her more in recent years than stem cell research, and none, I think, more clearly illustrates both her determination to make the Reagan legacy a living one and the courage with which she has approached that task.

Nancy didn't seek out this cause. It came to her through Doug Wick, the producer of **Gladiator** and **Stuart Little.** Wick's first boss in the movie industry was the director Alan Pakula, who had worked with Nancy during her movie days. His parents, Charles and Mary Jane Wick, are also close to the Reagans, but even though Doug is only half Nancy's age, the two of them have become fast friends, with Nancy serving as mentor on issues large and small.

"She's the best listener I have ever met," says Wick.

Doug remembers introducing Nancy to a parade of girlfriends back in the 1980s. Nancy kept her own counsel on most of them, but when Doug showed up at the White House with a new sweetheart named Lucy, the first lady could hold her tongue no longer. After giving Lucy a one-on-one tour of the White House, Nancy pulled the waiting boyfriend aside and let him have it with both barrels.

"Doug," she said, in no uncertain terms, "don't blow this one!"

He didn't. And later, after he finally popped the big question, he called his mom and dad. Then he called Nancy. It was Doug and Lucy's daughter, Tessa, was the reason Nancy confronted the issue of stem cell research.

When Tessa was diagnosed with Type 1 juvenile diabetes at age eight, she joined a million other kids unable to produce their own insulin, an essential hormone needed to transfer food into energy. After the shock wore off, Doug and Lucy did what any parents would do—they began to educate themselves on what waited ahead for Tessa in terms of symptoms and lifestyle changes, and on what possible remedies medical researchers were pursuing. A cure, they soon learned, meant more research, and more research meant lots more dollars. The Juvenile Diabetes Research Foundation International and other private groups were doing what they could, but the federal government is the eight-hundred-pound gorilla of medical research. Until Washington truly committed to finding a cure for juvenile diabetes, scientists were always going to play catch-up.

To lobby Congress for more research funding, Doug Wick launched an umbrella group called CuresNow. Then he turned to Nancy to help learn how to make his new organization work. Nancy stayed behind the scenes—that's her style—but she dove into the issue just as Reagan would have done, digesting everything she could read, calling doctors, talking with other mothers and fathers whose children had been saddled with the disease, and counseling Wick on how to open doors on Capitol Hill and which ones to concentrate on. Wick says that he was astounded at the reverence members of Congress and their staffs had for Nancy Reagan.

To give their mission national exposure, Doug and Lucy Wick decided to use the 1999 premiere of **Stuart Little** to call attention to juvenile diabetes. Nancy was invited and, as she rarely does, decided to leave her ailing husband to be by the Wicks' side. In the press line, she was lobbed the usual questions, but the one she decided to answer with gusto was the inquiry about why she was attending the opening.

"I'm here because I want to help my friend, Tessa Wick, who has juvenile diabetes," she said.

That's all it took. Wick was astounded at the calls his lobbying organization received over the next two days.

"It was a huge act of friendship," he said.

Nancy told Wick that her role would have to continue to be largely silent. "I am happy to give you all the advice I can," she said, "but that may be all I can give." By then, more was involved than her usual reluctance to take a lead role. Juvenile diabetes research had wandered into a political minefield.

The more Doug Wick talked with researchers, the more apparent it became that stem cells held perhaps the greatest promise for fashioning a cure for juvenile diabetes and a long list of other serious ailments, from heart disease to Parkinson's, various cancers, and Alzheimer's. Scientific proof was still lacking, but in test after test, the cells had shown an astounding capacity to regenerate neural pathways and damaged and diseased organs. The problem was procurement. Researchers had been harvesting stem cells from discarded human embryos, a practice vehemently opposed by many on the political right, including George W. Bush. To fortify their position, the anti-stem-cell crowd had bundled the issue with human cloning—a powerful one-two punch that threatened the nascent support the research was receiving in Congress.

Nancy was well aware that the pre-

Alzheimer's Ronald Reagan would quite likely have held the same reservations about stem cells, but the more she learned, the more she became convinced that this was one area where her husband's legacy would best be served by going beyond what might be thought of as original intent. After reading yet another article about how stem cells could help cure people like Tessa, Nancy called me in Washington and asked my advice about sending a letter to President Bush. She would frame it in terms of Reagan's disease, but she would be speaking for everyone who stood to benefit from the research. What did I think?

"Sure," I told her. "Pour your feelings into it. President Bush is a straight shooter just like you."

Nancy sent the following letter on April 11, 2001.

Dear Mr. President,

As you know, Ronnie recently celebrated his ninetieth birthday. In earlier times, we would have been able to share our mutual pride in a life filled with wonderful memories. Now, while I can draw strength from these memories, I do it alone as Ronnie struggles in a world un-

known to me or the scientists who devote their lives to Alzheimer's research. Because of this, I am determined to do what I can to save others from this pain and anguish. I'm writing, therefore, to ask your help in supporting what appears to be the most promising path to a cure—stem cell research.

I also know that this is not the first you have heard of this issue. And I know there are others who feel just as strongly in opposition to this. But I ask your help to ensure that this embryonic stem cell research, under appropriate guidelines, be protected as scientists pursue medical miracle possibilities.

Ronnie was very brave in writing to the public about his condition. It was his way of sharing with the thousands of families who are already afflicted. He always believed in man's ability to make this a better world and I know he would be gratified to know that his own suffering might spare others the same wrenching family journey.

Mr. President, I have some personal experience regarding the many decisions you face each day. I do not want to add to that burden, but I'd be very grateful if

you would take my thoughts and prayers into your consideration on this critical issue.

Most sincerely,
Nancy Reagan

Originally delivered to the White House and the congressional leadership, the letter began making the rounds on the Hill and the press within hours of its receipt. For Nancy, it was her first foray into a political brouhaha without her husband around to counsel her or bail her out. Having made the leap, she wasn't about to turn tail and run. She was much too respectful of the office of the president to bring the matter up with George and Laura Bush when she stayed at the White House as their guest in 2002, but she didn't pass up the chance to gently press the cause with White House staffers. Nor did she stop working the phones. Before long, Jerry Ford had joined the cause. Suddenly, stem cell research had the backing of all the living ex-Republican presidents whose name wasn't Bush!

When anti-stem-cell-research legislation sailed through the House of Representatives, Doug Wick and his team knew they had to bear down in the Senate. Once again, he asked for

Nancy's help, and once again, she gave it without reserve.

"I remember walking into John McCain's office," Wick told me. "As soon as I was inside the door, the senator said, 'Doug, I just got off the phone with Nancy. How can I help?' It was like that all the time. She was really forcing senators to learn more about the issue."

The education effort paid off. Early in 2003, Utah's Orrin Hatch—an old friend and supporter of both Reagans—introduced a bill that sought to clarify the complicated stem cell issue. Even though Hatch's bill would criminalize most forms of human cloning, it allowed limited therapeutic cloning on unfertilized human embryonic cells up to fourteen days old. Knowing that any deviation from 100 percent opposition to human cloning risked alienating the conservative Hatch's many friends in the pro-life community, Nancy decided to provide him some "air cover" in the form of a January 29 letter that the senator enlarged to a poster-size backdrop for the committee room.

The letter reads in part:

I'm writing . . . to offer my support for stem cell research and tell you I'm in favor of new legislation to allow the ethical

use of therapeutic cloning. Like you, I support a complete ban on reproductive cloning. However, I believe that embryonic stem cell research, under appropriate guidelines, may provide our scientists with many answers that are now beyond our grasp.

Orrin, there are so many diseases that can be cured, or at least helped, that we can't turn our back on this. We've lost so much time already. I can't bear to lose any more.

A few weeks after the letter was sent, I took a call from an irate member of Congress. "Reagan would never have approved of stem cell research," he shouted at me.

"Ronald Reagan," I replied, "didn't have to take care of Ronald Reagan for the last ten years." We agreed to disagree.

When Nancy is committed to something, she looks at the situation in black and white. There is no gray area to muddle things, and no turning back. President Bush has vowed to veto the Hatch bill if it makes it to his desk. Should it come to that, I'm sure Nancy will be disappointed, as will Doug and Lucy Wick and the hundreds of thousands of other parents whose children might benefit so greatly by this research, but I know, too, that so long as Nancy has fight in her, she won't give up on this quest.

It's an odd life Nancy leads these days, balanced between public honors and the long quiet times with Reagan. More and more, the world around her shrinks. The rare love that the Reagans shared, the partnership that made them both so much more than they would have been alone, is one-sided now. Nancy has to handle the daily decisions and larger ones.

The loneliest, toughest decision she had to make was selling their beloved Rancho del Cielo. Reagan had paid about half a million dollars back in 1974 for the nearly seven-hundred-acre spread in the Santa Barbara foothills, the best money he ever spent.

"This place casts a spell," he would later explain. "I suppose it's the scriptural line, 'I look to the hills from whence cometh my strength.' I understand it better when I'm up here." No wonder they both thought of it as their private piece of heaven.

Rancho del Cielo was full of memories for both of them: Nancy in her dirty blue jeans, a cowboy shirt, and a straw hat, maybe paint splattered on her face—so much different from her public image and always, it seemed, so happy. Nancy learned to ride at the ranch, on No-Strings, the horse her husband had given her. On the Reagans' twenty-fifth wedding anniversary, Reagan reproposed to Nancy in a canoe on the gentle waters of Lake Lucky—the pond where he had once snatched up black snakes and which he later christened with one of Edie Davis's nicknames.

No wonder Nancy felt that, of all places, Reagan would still feel at home at the ranch, even as Alzheimer's advanced on him, but that wasn't the case. The long ride to the ranch from Bel Air confused him, and the surroundings that had done so much to reinvigorate him when he was president became unfamiliar. On top of it all, Nancy knew that she simply couldn't afford to keep up both the ranch and the Bel Air home. The nursing bills and the cost of maintaining a single comfortable residence for her husband would be strain enough on the budget, especially since no one can predict how long Alzheimer's will hold victims in its grip. Aware of Nancy's feelings, California governor Pete Wilson tried to get Congress to make the ranch a national landmark. When that failed, Nancy put it on the market. Happily, the ranch ended up being purchased by the Young America's Foundation, which will use it to teach future generations about the fortieth president.

Nancy spent her last day at the ranch gathering souvenirs and taking the western paintings down off the wall. She packed up the tack room from the barn and paid a last visit to the pet graveyard to bid a final good-bye to all the dogs that have lived with them over the years. She told me it was one of the saddest days of her life, and the longest ride home from Rancho del Cielo she ever had.

There are plenty of good moments, though— times when she gets to proudly bear her husband's banner, other times (and increasingly so) when she is the one being honored. On July 10, 2002, George W. Bush bestowed the Presidential Medal of Freedom on Nancy and twelve other distinguished Americans. Bush cited particularly Nancy's work combating drug and alcohol abuse and her promotion of the Foster Grandparents Program. Established by Harry S. Truman in 1945 to recognize civilians for service during World War II and reinstated in 1963 by Jack Kennedy to honor distinguished service, the medal is the nation's highest civilian award.

A few months earlier, Nancy was again at President Bush's side, this time to receive a Congressional Gold Medal issued jointly to Ronald and Nancy Reagan. Bush first praised Ronald Reagan's leadership. Then he turned to Nancy:

At every step of an amazing life, Nancy Reagan has been at Ronald Reagan's side. As his optimism inspired us, her love and devotion strengthen him. As first lady of California, Mrs. Reagan spoke out on behalf of POWs and American servicemen missing in action. As our first lady of the United States, Nancy Reagan led an antidrug campaign that helped significantly reduce teen drug use. Now she has joined the fight against Alzheimer's.

Nancy knows she can do only so much, but she is determined not to do less than she can. She has established the Ronald and Nancy Reagan Research Institute, as part of the Chicago-based Alzheimer's Association, to help fund start-up work on new initiatives to find a cure. The Ronald and Nancy Reagan Family Fund, part of the local Alzheimer's Association in Santa Barbara, provides money for what so many families stricken by the disease can't afford: caregiving of various sorts as well as respites for the family members who provide it. Nancy has also funded a research project at the Mayo Clinic in both their names.

She has made sure, too, that the Reagan legacy will live on through the Reagan Library in Simi Valley, California. It is a temple to the greatness of the man, but it would not be the monument it is without the dedication of Nancy Reagan. Nancy spends an enormous amount of time

working there, signing books, arranging confer-
ences, and attending fund-raisers and board
meetings. After all, it's not just history that she's
keeping an eye on. Just as she has been doing for
a half century, Nancy Reagan is watching out for
the love of her life.

6

HER FINEST HOUR

Ronald Reagan always told me that there was a reason for everything. Back in the 1970s, when we lost the Proposition 1 campaign to limit property taxes in California, he reassured all of us fatigued and depressed supporters that something bigger was at play. (And, of course, he was right.) He did the same thing—and was right again—in 1976 when he came up short in his historic effort to wrest the nomination from fellow Republican Gerald Ford, the incumbent president. Likewise in 1981, as he was recovering in George Washington University Hospital from the near-fatal attempt on his life, the president took me aside to tell me that he was certain he had been "spared for a reason."

"There's a plan and someday we'll all understand," he said.

If it were still possible for Ronald Reagan to reason at all anymore, I believe he would feel the same way about the terrible disease that has robbed him of so much of the last decade: it's part of the plan, he would say, a chance for his beloved Nancy to step out from his shadow and let history take another look at her and her accomplishments. In fact, I can just hear him now: "Maybe with me off the stage, people will get a chance to see the same wonderful qualities I've been seeing for the last fifty years." Just as it was all about Reagan with her, so it was all about Nancy with him.

The first time I got to see close up just how much Nancy meant to him was in February 1967, in the capitol at Sacramento. I've told this story so many times that I hesitate to repeat it here, but nothing could be more emblematic of the bond between them than what I saw that day.

I had appeared a few minutes early for a meeting the governor convened with three assemblymen from northern California. They were—not surprisingly—a few minutes late, but Reagan could have cared less. He greeted me with a warm smile and offered a cup of coffee. Armed with caffeine, I moved toward his large desk and took the seat reserved for staff. He was ambling back around the desk to his own side when the intercom announced that his wife was on the line. Immediately, he spun on one heel and darted to his phone, like a thirsty man to a frosty glass of water. As he sunk into the leather chair,

he greeted her with a slow, drawn-out "Hel-
looo." I stood up to leave, caught in a private
moment between this most private of couples,
but the governor would have none of it.

Nonsense, the look on his face said. He then
guided me back to my seat with his body language and raised an index finger, silently indicat-
ing that this call would be a quickie.

I reviewed my notes as they talked, looking up
only when I heard Reagan say "good-bye." He
was sitting erect in his chair. As I watched, he listened for a second more, then leaned slightly
closer to the phone's cradle and offered up another, somewhat softer "good-bye." Amazingly,
that wasn't the end of it. Five or six more "good-
bye's" followed until the governor's head was
nearly resting on the phone cradle. Finally, with
one last "bye," no more really than a puff of
wind, he hung the phone up as carefully as if it
were made of the finest crystal. Then he looked
up at me and winked.

I began to say something, but he gently cut me
off as only he could do.

"You know, it's funny, but neither of us ever
wants to be the last one to say 'good-bye.'"

Now, the choice has been made. Alzheimer's
has given Nancy the last—and painfully long—
good-bye. I think back to all of the times I've
seen them holding hands or hugging. For so
many politicians, a spouse seems to be a kind of

necessary appendage, someone to sit beside you at the head table or attest to your virtue and commitment to family values. That was never the case with Nancy and Ron. If Ronald Reagan and I were at a reception somewhere in the middle of a sea of people, and I saw his eyes light up with a pure sparkle, I knew exactly what had happened: he had just seen his Nancy walking into the room.

She was the source of his happiness, the one who made him such a perfectly contented man. For all any of us can really know, she might still be.

For many reasons, this has been the hardest chapter for me to complete. Few diseases are harsher than Alzheimer's. At a time in life when the body tires and solace comes so much from old memories, memory itself atrophies and disappears. As I sit here, Ronald Reagan is ninety-two years old, no pup to be sure, but even though he was the oldest of our presidents, he was always one of the most vital. It is a cruel trick that such a vibrant, larger-than-life guy like Reagan is forced to go out this way. But it's not just Ronald Reagan who had his future shortchanged by his disease. Nancy did, too. For a woman who always received her strength from his love and energy, this is a terrible way to end up their life together.

In a previous book, I described my last visit with Ronald Reagan, back in 1997 at his post-presidency office in Los Angeles. His disease was progressing, and Nancy was circling the wagons. Soon, only family and those who were tending to the president would be allowed to see him. I'd come, really, to say good-bye to a man I love, a man I stood beside and served for the most meaningful years of my life. I didn't know how I would find the words, but I wanted to say them.

He looked great when I opened the door and stepped in—a blue suit, flawless French cuffs, just the right tie—but it didn't take long to realize that Ronald Reagan had no idea who I was, or any interest in why I had walked into his office. A book was in his hands; his attention to it was total. Finally, I slipped over to his side to see what it was. He was reading a picture book about Traveler, Robert E. Lee's famous horse. I was heartbroken.

Things have gone sharply downhill in the years since. Nancy tells me some of the story; his doctors and others have told me more. I won't include the grim details here. Alzheimer's does enough to rob dignity, for its victim and for those around him or her, without adding more insult to the almost unbearable injury of the disease. Those with loved ones who have suffered similarly can fill in the picture; those who haven't just need to imagine the worst. Suffice it to say that a man who has done so much for America can now do so little for himself.

While she wants, as always, to protect Reagan's memory, Nancy did ask me to include as much about the disease as I could so readers could better understand what is happening to so many Alzheimer's families who must struggle in silence and anonymity. The first place I went for answers was to the people who know the disease best: the Alzheimer's Association, an organization that Nancy Reagan helped put on the map.

Alzheimer's disease is only one of many disorders that cause the gradual loss of brain cells, but it has a shocking growth curve. Once considered rare, Alzheimer's is now the number one cause of dementia, a catchall term for a decline in thinking and memory skills. Symptoms include a gradual loss of retention, problems with reasoning or judgment, disorientation, difficulty in learning, loss of speaking skills, and a decline in the ability to perform basic and routine tasks. Related diseases like Parkinson's and Huntington's share a common, horrible element with Alzheimer's: they destroy the brain.

Alzheimer's has its own timetable, depending on its victim. The duration can be from three to twenty years. Memory is the first to go, but as the disease progresses, it attacks cells in other regions of the brain. If a patient lives long enough, he or she will need complete and comprehensive care. In the absence of any other serious illness, the loss of the brain function will eventually cause death. Ronald Reagan is in his ninth year with Alzheimer's, a long survival time for a man already in his nineties. The doctors tell me his physical stamina and healthy lifestyle are probably responsible for this resistance.

As the experts know—and Nancy is unfortunately one of them now—Alzheimer's does not sneak up on its victims without warning. It sends quiet, seemingly innocuous signals. Identifying these signals early will not stem Alzheimer's progress. That's another of the disease's cruelties. But it can help families prepare better for what lies ahead. The Alzheimer's Association has identified nine warning signs that a loved one could be at risk of the disease.

- The first is memory loss, one of the most common early symptoms. While we expect older people to forget minor things like dates and names, those edging into Alzheimer's forget more things more often and never recall them afterward.
- People with dementia often find it hard to complete everyday tasks that are so familiar we often don't even think about how to do them. A person with Alzheimer's disease might not know the steps for preparing a meal, using an electric razor, or tying a tie.
- Although everyone has trouble finding the right word from time to time, a person with

Alzheimer's more often than not forgets simple words or substitutes such unusual ones that conversation or correspondence can be hard to follow. Instead of asking for a toothbrush, the Alzheimer's Association points out, the disease's victims might ask for "that thing for my mouth."

- Disorientation is the fourth warning sign, and a big problem. People with Alzheimer's disease can become lost on their own street or in their own neighborhood, forgetting where they are and how they got there. The scariest part is they don't know how to get back home.

- Judgment disappears next. Victims often dress without thinking about the weather, wearing layers of clothes on hot days and a pair of shorts on the coldest. Or a meticulous woman might come downstairs to greet company wearing only her underclothes. Alzheimer's victims often lose all idea of the value of money, making them easy prey for telemarketers or for door-to-door salespeople who convince them to buy goods or services they simply don't need.

- After judgment comes the decline of abstract thinking. Balancing a checkbook turns into an impossible chore because victims have forgotten what numbers are and how to use them.

- Losing things becomes second nature for Alzheimer's patients. They put wineglasses in

the medicine cabinet or lightbulbs in the
freezer.
- Mood swings become commonplace, too. All
of us have highs and lows, but Alzheimer's
victims have much more rapid mood swings
for no apparent reason. Once-steady people
can turn on a dime, becoming extremely
confused, suspicious, fearful, or dependent on
a loved one. Sadly, they sometimes drive away
the people they most need to depend on as the
disease progresses.
- The final sign the Alzheimer's Association
warns of is loss of initiative. Even in the
early stages of the disease, victims may
become extremely passive, sitting in front of
the television for hours, sleeping too much,
and taking a pass on once favorite activities.

These warning signals, I should point out, are
just that: flags to alert you to get help for a loved
one. As noted earlier, there is no cure, at least not
yet, but early diagnosis of Alzheimer's disease or
other disorders causing dementia is an important
step in getting the right treatment.

Nancy has also taught me what Alzheimer's
isn't.

Like most people, I always believed memory
loss to be a natural part of the aging process.
Every family has enshrined in its private mythol-
ogy the great-aunt who couldn't remember her

own name. Belovedly daffy, she might have been, but experts now see severe memory loss as a symptom of serious illness.

Most of us believe Alzheimer's disease to be hereditary, and to some extent it is, but to a far lesser extent than I had realized. A rare manifestation known as early-onset Alzheimer's, affecting middle-aged people, has been linked to three different genes that can predict with high accuracy the onset of the disease. Scientists have also found one gene associated with an increased risk of the far more common late-onset Alzheimer's, and they know from studies that a person has a greater risk of developing the disease if he or she has an immediate parent or sibling who was an Alzheimer's victim. But the greatest risk factor for developing late-onset Alzheimer's disease is simply getting old.

Before Ronald Reagan's was diagnosed, I didn't know Alzheimer's was a death knell, either. A few government-approved drugs might temporarily improve or stabilize memory and thinking skills in some people, but the truth is that once it takes hold, Alzheimer's is like a powerful army that marches right on through whatever barricades you might throw up against it. To be sure, many of its victims never get to that point. They're carried off first by other diseases, some of them grown opportunistic as Alzheimer's erodes the body's capacity to perform basic operations. For the families of those who do die of the disease, the death knell might not be an unwelcome sound. That's a question I've never dared to ask Nancy: would her husband be better off dead? But my guess is that Nancy's devotion to Reagan is so total and the communion between them still so mystical and deep that even a faint light is better than no light at all.

People have tried to identify external factors such as artificial sweeteners and even aluminum as triggering agents for Alzheimer's disease. When I first heard about the rumored link to sweeteners, I thought immediately of the fake ballpoint pen filled with NutraSweet that Reagan always carried with him. He loved to show it off, pulling it out of his pocket with a flourish, then clicking the top twice to shoot out the sweetener for his Sanka. But from what the experts tell me, tossing out the NutraSweet won't make a difference. Nor will getting rid of aluminum cans, pots, and pans. At least so far as anyone has proven up to this point.

I remember as if it were yesterday the exact moment I first realized something was wrong with my old boss. I had arranged an appointment with Reagan for a pair of producers working on an HBO documentary. They were a rare breed—Hollywood Republicans!—and they were dying to meet the Gipper. He graciously accepted, and we set the gathering for his Century

City office. The president was in good spirits and looked typically wonderful in his dark navy suit and red tie.

After some boilerplate small talk about L.A. traffic, one of the producers asked the president about his undying optimism: How did you keep smiling during those tough times in the first administration? Reagan got this softball all the time, and he had a story in response that never failed to get a laugh—a wonderful yarn about twin brothers. One is shown a room full of new toys and begins crying, knowing that most of them will break eventually. The other is led to a barn full to the rafters with manure and gleefully starts shoveling away because "with all that manure, there's got to be a pony in here somewhere!" I began to grin in anticipation, but the story never arrived. Instead, the president stammered something about always trying to keep a "healthy outlook."

Shocked, I prodded him. "Mr. President, tell the one about the kid and the pony."

"Which one's that?" he responded.

Incredulous, I pressed him again. "The one you've told a million times—about the toys and the barn full of manure."

The lost look on Reagan's face told me to move on. To cover his embarrassment, I quickly related the story myself, to the usual amusement, including a hearty chuckle from my old boss, who once owned the story and now was laughing as if he were hearing it for the first time. The moment passed, the meeting moved on, but clearly something was wrong. Whether it was temporary or permanent, I didn't know—and I didn't know then what to call the condition if it was permanent—but I decided I couldn't ignore what I had just witnessed.

I had kept in close touch with the president in the five years since he had left the Oval Office, but I'd kept in closer touch with Nancy. Even now that any official connection had long since ceased, we seemed to be each other's telephone habit, so I called to tell her about the meeting. I remember wondering as I was waiting for her to come on the line why she hadn't mentioned Reagan's memory loss. Surely, this couldn't have been the first instance, and she was constantly monitoring his health and condition. It wasn't long before I had my answer: Nancy's protective instincts, always strong, were raging.

Nancy had been seeing more and more of these moments of lapsed memory and inexplicable behavior. Adding to her concern was the fact that she felt she couldn't discuss the matter with anyone. One small leak to the press, and the media would begin homing in on the ex-president, testing him at every turn. The Reagans were already booked in for their annual physicals at the Mayo Clinic in Minnesota, more than half a year down the road. I'm sure that if Nancy had suspected Alzheimer's, she would have insisted on moving the date up dramatically, but to her, he seemed to be suffering from not much more than old age. Until she could get Reagan to the clinic and let the doctors determine if something worse was ailing him, Nancy would go into full gear to control his schedule and public appearances. As hard as she tried, though, it wasn't enough.

The most telling single incident happened in February 1994, and it would unleash a chain of events that would eventually take Ronald Reagan out of the public spotlight forever, away even from longtime friends like me.

For Reagan's eighty-fourth birthday, the Republican National Committee planned a major Washington celebration to salute the former commander in chief. RNC chairman Haley Barbour pulled out all the stops for the event, including an appearance by Margaret Thatcher, who would both introduce the former president and offer high praise for the Reagan Revolution.

On the way to Washington, the Reagans stopped in New York for an informal event in the city, the sort of schmoozing that Reagan in his prime made look effortless. Nancy would later ascribe the problems to a "bad case of jet lag," but she knew in her heart that wasn't the answer.

"He wasn't himself in New York," she told me later. "Something was terribly wrong."

Nancy knew better than anyone that if Reagan didn't snap out of it by that evening in Washington, the rumor mill would begin humming. This was the president's first high-profile visit to the nation's capital in years, and it wasn't the friendly territory it had been back in the 1980s. The Reagan record was under sharp attack by the Clinton White House, and the press would be watching to see if the former president would return fire. Obviously, it was a terrible time for Reagan to have come down with something, whatever it was. Hundreds of Reagan loyalists had been looking forward to this for months, many traveling great distances to attend. They wanted to honor the Gipper.

A few hours before the Washington speech, Nancy pulled Fred Ryan into her room and told him her concerns. Fred had been with the president since the early days of the White House, and Nancy had grown to trust him completely. I did, too. I'd given Fred his first major assignment in the Reagan White House in 1981, making him head of presidential scheduling, a responsibility I obviously feel is huge and one that he handled with great skill. Later, after I left the administration, he was named assistant to the president, the highest rank in the White House. When it came time to leave Washington in January 1989, Fred managed the departure and the setup of the Reagans' new life in California. He had been their

principal staff and adviser since the Reagans returned to private life.

When Nancy approached Fred with a worried
look on her face, he knew instantly what she was
talking about. Fred had been the first person I
spoke with after leaving Reagan's office, following the failed-joke incident. He told me then that
he had observed similar incidents. When we
talked later on the subject, he said as Nancy did
that they were waiting to get Reagan to the clinic
for a comprehensive examination.

Nancy and Fred agreed that they could not
cancel the birthday celebration or rob the atten-
dees of their guest of honor. Instead, they
would have to try to protect the president both
before and after his speech. Fred knew just how
tough that was going to be. He had been fielding
calls for weeks from friends and former White
House staffers, begging for a little quality time
with the president, maybe even a one-on-one.
Telling them now that their promised three minutes wasn't going to happen would raise tem-
peratures to the boiling point, but he and Nancy
went ahead nonetheless and drew a circle
around the president, keeping him cloistered in
a holding room before his speech and rushing
him off to his hotel afterward. (Secret Service
agents can come in handy if you're trying to
keep people away.) The results were predictable.
It was the maddest old friends of the president

had ever been, Fred told me. "People were really frosted."

When it came time for Reagan's entrance, the Gipper handled himself with his usual class, taking his seat to the right of host Haley Barbour, with Nancy by his other side. Across the dais sat Lady Thatcher and her husband. The Reagans looked as if they had just hopped off the top of a wedding cake, with Reagan in black tie.

Always a favorite of the Reagan Right, Maggie Thatcher warmed up the crowd, taking listeners on a trip down memory lane, reminding them what Reagan had done not just for America but for the world. The president looked on as he always did at such moments, with a kind of shy, "aw shucks" smile. Beside him, Nancy's pleasant facade masked a dread of the unknown. Never before had she had this feeling of unease before a major speech. Reagan was the Great Communicator, after all, but now age, fatigue, flu, jet lag, and perhaps something worse—maybe far worse— had conspired against her husband on this most special of evenings.

As Thatcher finished her remarks, she beckoned to Reagan to take over the lectern. He walked gently to the microphone and hugged the Iron Lady to a cascade of applause. Love and warmth overflowed the ballroom.

What happened next startled those of us who had known Reagan the longest and seen him perform impeccably at dozens upon dozens of such events. Under the klieg lights, he suddenly looked every one of his eighty-four years. Although there were TelePrompTers on hand, Reagan began to search the left side of his tuxedo jacket for notes. From where I sat, he seemed to be having trouble digging his usual three-by-five index cards out of his pocket. I noticed Nancy looking down to her plate, deeply concerned. As the applause died down, Reagan began talking very, very slowly, looking down at his notes, ignoring the rolling TelePrompTer in front of him. It was a recipe for confusion.

His speech was stunted. "I . . . am . . . so . . . happy . . . to . . . be . . . here . . ."

This was not the man Nancy knew, not the man any of us who had been with him so long knew. "I . . . was . . . afraid . . . that . . . you . . . would . . . not . . . recognize . . . me." We almost didn't.

It went on this way for a few more long moments until the Gipper finally reverted to his old self and the tension began to dissipate. Rising slowly—like a goose taking off for flight—he took a few gentle jabs at the Arkansan in the White House, told a risqué political joke, and as usual left them wanting more. The meandering at the start of the speech had lasted only a minute or two, but to Nancy, it was a lifetime. Most of those in attendance, I'm sure, dismissed

the opening stumble as an understandable conse-
quence of age. But Nancy knew better. Something bigger was happening.

Back at the hotel, the first thing Reagan said
was "I guess I'm confused." He had a blank look
on his face.

As he finished, Nancy gently took him by the
hand. "Come on, honey," she told him. "Get into
your pajamas and lie down for a while. You're
tired."

Obligingly, Reagan went into the bedroom
with her. As he was changing into his night-
clothes, Nancy came back to the living room and
huddled with Reagan's personal physician, John
Hutton, and Fred Ryan. Hutton, who had been
Reagan's doctor since the second term in the
White House, was clearly concerned. "Some
people become stuck in a moment of confusion
like that and never come out," he told me later.
But that wasn't to be the case this night. As the
three of them were talking, Reagan emerged
from his bedroom seeming perfectly normal.
Hutton recalls being amazed at Reagan's quick
turnaround. "Nancy took him into the bedroom,
and ten minutes later he came out, cleaned up, in
his pajamas and looking like his old self."

When Reagan again went back to the bedroom, this time to retire for the night, Nancy
continued her discussion with Hutton and Ryan.
They agreed that during the scheduled Mayo

Clinic visit that summer, more work should be done to examine the president's mental faculties to see if anything was amiss other than simply aging. Hutton remembers that Nancy was stoic and composed as they talked, asking lots of questions about what could be wrong. The one subject she returned to time and again was a horse riding accident that her husband had suffered a few years earlier at the Mexico ranch of Reagan friend Bill Wilson. There was no known link then between brain trauma and an increased risk of Alzheimer's, but Nancy was convinced that getting thrown had something to do with his faltering faculties, and in fact, subsequent studies have shown that Alzheimer's is more common in people who have sustained a severe head injury coupled with a loss of consciousness.

Hutton knew well what riding accident Nancy was talking about. He had been at the Wilson ranch when it happened. John went everywhere with Reagan, along with a small Secret Service contingent—perquisites enjoyed by all ex-presidents. He later told me that the throw would have been a bad one even for a man half Reagan's age. The president was literally tossed over the horse's head and knocked unconscious. He lay motionless, flat on his back, before recovering his senses. Back at the ranch, he insisted he was fine, but two weeks later he complained of a spinning head. That's when Nancy insisted that a CAT scan be ordered. Hutton and Reagan both agreed, and in due course the doctors located what amounted basically to a blood blister on the president's brain.

"Maybe Sam Donaldson was right," Reagan cracked when he got the word. "I do have a hole in my head."

It was funny then, another sign of his amazing resilience. But after New York and Washington, Nancy was no longer laughing so easily. She and Hutton agreed to wait until the August checkup at the Mayo Clinic before making drastic decisions. Maybe, they thought, they were just overreacting. Still, she began to silently count the days leading up to the Mayo visit.

As always, the Reagans reported together to the clinic at 8 A.M. and then were led to separate quarters for testing and evaluation. This time, though, John Hutton had alerted the Mayo doctors that Reagan was suffering from bouts of memory loss and confusion, and the clinic had beefed up the neurological portion of the exam. Over several hours, the doctors checked for a murderer's row of potential ailments from brain tumors to chemical imbalances and more, eliminating each with a different test. It's virtually impossible to diagnose Alzheimer's with absolute certainty—only an autopsy can do that—but by the time they were through, the Mayo doctors were fairly confident that Reagan was in the early stages of the disease.

The next morning, when the medical team met with the Reagans, they told the former president that he was suffering from "memory loss beyond age appropriate. . . . We think you have the beginnings of Alzheimer's."

Reagan's response, Nancy recalls, was characteristically lacking in self-pity. "Okay, what do we do now?" she remembers him asking.

"This can be slow or fast," the doctors told him. "We can't tell how it will progress, but you will eventually lose most of your short-term memory."

For the old Ronald Reagan, a line like that would have been the perfect lead-in to a moment of relieving humor, but Nancy remembers him just sitting there, taking it in as his future was being spelled out in such grim terms. For her part, she says, "I knew it was something, and of course, I thought it had do with the accident, the horse, but I had no idea it was Alzheimer's. And I certainly did not know what that meant."

She would soon find out.

Back in California, one of the first calls Nancy made was to Casey Ribicoff. Casey's husband, Abe, the former Connecticut governor and senator, was in the advanced stages of the disease, and Casey was his primary caregiver. The two women had first been introduced by the legendary social butterfly Jerome "The Zipper" Zipkin, but they were never really more than casual acquaintances until that moment. Within months, they would be the closest of friends. Indeed, if Nancy has a double in this world, Casey might be it.

Casey told Nancy of the many difficulties that she would face. "You can't leave him in anyone else's hands without writing down a lengthy list of 'in case of emergency' phone numbers," she told Nancy. Because Abe had little use for sleep, Casey went on, she got precious little herself. Casey ended up that first conversation with a suggested reading list. For Nancy, it was the beginning of an education that continues to this day.

"There isn't just one book you can read on this," she told me not long ago, a decade into her learning curve. "You just have to take it one day at a time. I had no idea back then there was going to be ten years of this."

Nancy needed only a few calls with Casey to realize that her life as she knew it was essentially over. Unlike the Ribicoffs, indeed unlike any other family struck by this terrible disease, the Reagans could count on a devoted Secret Service contingent to help out. There would be no question of getting the best medical care or access to the newest treatment protocols, but Nancy re-

membered the words of the minister who married them: "for better or for worse." The worst,
or close to it, had just arrived with a bang. From
this moment forward, she would spend every
minute making sure Reagan was protected and
comfortable for the rest of his life.

One of the first questions Nancy had to deal
with was who to tell and how—and how much—
to tell them. Perhaps Reagan could live out his
years without breaking the news to the outside
world at all, or at least directly. His public appearances would become fewer and fewer, and
far more controlled: a stand-up, a wave, that famous smile, all seen from an increasingly remote
distance. The Secret Service agents could help
with that, and they were sure to be an effective
way to keep people at bay once the disease had
him fully in its grip. Nancy could then take care
of her husband in her own way, on her timetable.
It would be just the two of us, Nancy thought.
Does anybody beyond the immediate family and
close friends and aides really need to know?

Even as she asked herself such questions,
though, Nancy knew the answer. Officially, ex-
presidents are private citizens, but they're far
closer to public trusts. At the White House and
in Sacramento, Nancy had also learned what
every politician and every political spouse ultimately realizes: there is no such thing as an air-
tight secret. Leaks happen.

A few days after the Reagans had returned to California, Nancy and Fred Ryan, with whom she had been sharing these worries, decided to put the question directly to the president himself. They were sitting in the living room of the Bel Air house, Fred told me later. Reagan seemed completely in charge of his faculties. It was a good moment to broach the subject.

Always direct, Nancy turned to her husband and said, "We're going to have to deal with this, Ronnie. Word is going to get out. We need to think about this."

Nancy and Fred kicked the subject around for a little while longer before Reagan joined in. Once again, he cut straight to the chase.

"Okay," he said, "how do we tell people about this?"

Assuming the president was talking about the fairly small, family-like staff of the Reagan library and foundation, Fred suggested a personal letter that could be photocopied and handed out.

Reagan nodded, then stood and walked off to his desk in the private study.

As Reagan wrote, Nancy and Fred looked at Reagan's calendar to see what events should be scrubbed, changed, or kept on. The Mayo Clinic doctors had advised against putting Reagan in situations where he could be easily confused or embarrassed by what could be a fairly speedy decline in memory. Reagan's traditional Christmas visit to a local children's hospital and an event at the Ronald Reagan Library both were coming up within the next three months. Would he be up to the challenge by then?

Nancy and Fred Ryan were still reviewing the schedule fifteen minutes later when Reagan came back carrying a two-page, handwritten note.

"Honey, what do you think?" he asked, handing the paper to Nancy.

Nancy sat on the sofa, reading the letter, or trying to—her eyes filled with tears, she says, almost immediately. When she was through, she nodded quietly and passed the note back to her husband. Almost immediately, he handed the note off to Ryan.

Just as Reagan was about to let go of the document, he pulled it back from Ryan's waiting hand, sat down, and scratched out two words with a thick, black mark, then added another word more to his preference. Reagan's blackout did a good job of concealing. Even today, Nancy has no idea what words he edited out at the last moment. Nobody thought to ask then. Now, it's too late.

As both Fred and Nancy had seen, the letter was addressed to "My Fellow Americans." This was not going to be a private missive to friends and staff. As always, the Reagans would be open about their new plight.

My Fellow Americans,

I have recently been told that I am one of the millions of Americans who will be afflicted with Alzheimer's disease.

Upon learning this news, Nancy and I had to decide whether as private citizens we would keep this a private matter or whether we would make this news known in a public way.

In the past Nancy suffered from breast cancer and I had my cancer surgeries. We found through our open disclosures we were able to raise public awareness. We were happy that as a result many more people underwent testing. They were treated in early stages and able to return to normal, healthy lives.

So now, we feel it is important to share it with you. In opening our hearts, we hope this might promote a greater awareness of this condition. Perhaps it will encourage a clearer understanding of the individuals and families who are affected by it.

At the moment I feel just fine. I intend to live the remainder of the years God gives me on this earth doing the things I have always done. I will continue to share life's journey with my beloved Nancy and

my family. I plan to enjoy the great out-
doors and stay in touch with my friends
and supporters.

Unfortunately, as Alzheimer's disease
progresses, the family often bears a
heavy burden. I only wish there was some
way I could spare Nancy from this
painful experience. When the time
comes, I am confident that with your help
she will face it with faith and courage.

In closing let me thank you, the American people, for giving me the great honor
of allowing me to serve as your president. When the Lord calls me home
whenever that may be, I will leave with
the greatest love for this country of ours
and eternal optimism for its future.

I now begin the journey that will lead
me into the sunset of my life. I know that
for America there will always be a bright
dawn ahead.

Thank you my friends. May God always bless you.

Sincerely,
Ronald Reagan

In retrospect, of course, it only makes sense that
Ronald Reagan would choose to take what

amounted almost to his death sentence public. As he notes in the letter, he and Nancy were consistently out front whenever some new physical crisis threatened, especially for people who were accused of bringing Hollywood-style vanity to the political arena. Even the small depredations of age were handled head-on.

Believe me, there's not a political consultant in the world who likes to see his client wearing a hearing aid. Hearing aids say **old** and **tired** to the electorate. But when Reagan was forced to get a hearing aid while still in the White House, he wore it proudly, and ear doctors the world over reported increased visits from the president's contemporaries. For Reagan, it was simply a matter of being handed lemons and trying to make some lemonade out of them: if I have to wear one of the damn things, I might as well do some good in the process. I used to laugh in the Oval Office whenever I began to hear the telltale high-pitched ring that meant the president had cranked his hearing aid up too high. He couldn't hear the ring, of course, but his staff sure could. It never bothered him when I alerted him to the noise; he would simply adjust the volume and go on with the meeting.

Now, facing a fate so far more serious than losing his hearing, Reagan wasn't going to falter. It was time to get the word out, not just to intimates or to longtime staff but to everyone. As

Nancy told me years later, "Why wouldn't he have done so? We always did it that way." Nor was he going to ponder long and hard on the rightness of his decision. As Fred Ryan and Nancy looked on, the president rose from his chair with a quick slap of his hands and announced, "I'm going to the ranch."

With a Secret Service contingent driving Reagan to Rancho del Cielo, Nancy decided to place a conference call to the Ronald Reagan Library board of directors: a who's who of Reagan insiders ranging from movie mogul Lew Wasserman to former secretary of state George Shultz and media billionaire Walter Annenberg.

The dozen luminaries whom Fred Ryan got on the line expected the president to come on personally and make a pitch to raise funds for the library or another like-minded cause. Everyone knew he was failing to one extent or another, but the group had sat in on calls like these many times before. Instead, Nancy asked Fred to read the letter verbatim.

It was quiet for what seemed an entire minute afterward. Then these closest of friends began to speak straight from the heart.

"What a great American," said one.

"I can't believe it," said another.

Then Wasserman softly, slowly asked the questions I was thinking. "Nancy, where is he now? Is he okay?"

Shultz added, "Yes, my God, how is he holding up? What hospital is he in?"

There was a slight pause before Nancy responded. "Actually, he just went to the ranch."

More stunned silence followed. The ranch? Was that possible? This was new territory for everybody. None of us knew how to react or what to do next. After all, at the time, he was the most prominent citizen to ever announce such an ailment in such a way. It was vintage Reagan, and vintage of him, too, to leave it up to Nancy to inform us and orchestrate the public release of the letter. He instinctively trusted Nancy to figure out how to handle the onslaught.

Fred phoned me immediately after the conference call, and I in turn called Nancy. She was subdued and very cautious in what she said. This was new ground for her, as well. The less said, she felt, the better. A few weeks later, I was quoted saying that Reagan's brother and mother both suffered from some sort of dementia. I had the facts on my side, but Nancy still phoned me in a semi-rage.

"Why did you say that? Where did you get your information?" she demanded, even though she knew I was right. "I don't want anybody talking about this. I'm doing everything I can to protect Ronnie, and I don't need friends of his giving opinions to the papers."

The message was clear: **Don't talk about this.** It would take a full year or more before she became more open about the disease, but I had no sooner hung the phone up than I understood Nancy's anger. Here she was trying to get her hands around this new, unpleasant thing and I was out yapping to the press. **Let me handle this,** was her message. And she was right: they were the ones who would have to decide what to say and when to say it, not me.

The day the letter was made public, President Clinton was in California. Soon, he was going on at every turn about Reagan's newly disclosed condition, pulling out the organ stops as only he can do. In Bel Air, Nancy found herself fielding calls from Reagan partisans all around the country, expressing dismay that Clinton was the guy breaking the news to the world. It wasn't long, too, before more powerful parties began to phone.

Nancy sat dutifully by the phone all that day, fielding calls from heads of state, kings and queens, senators, members of Congress, past and present cabinet members, old Hollywood pals and staff. As Reagan cleared brush at Rancho del Cielo, Nancy was reading the letter twice—and slowly—to a concerned, fascinated President Hosni Mubarak of Egypt. Time and again, she assured the famous and the less so that her husband was doing fine, then guardedly tried to explain the details of this misunderstood condition called Alzheimer's.

For those of us closest to Nancy and Ronald

Reagan, the announcement was particularly dramatic stuff. The line was being drawn. From now on, access to the president would be sharply limited. We all knew there was a time coming when "limited" would yield to "curtailed." Always her husband's gatekeeper—even when others of us theoretically controlled the schedule—Nancy would become his public face and final custodian.

Since my last visit with Ronald Reagan in 1997, I have been forced to watch his decline from a respectful distance. For more than thirty years I was as close to him as I was to my own father and brother—and he filled parts of both roles for me. I used to sometimes daydream about the good times Carolyn and I would have with the Reagans after all the hullabaloo of public office was over: a chance to sit back and reminisce in tranquillity about all we had been through. Instead, like Reagan's other old, close friends from Hollywood, Sacramento, and Washington, I've had to sit on the sidelines as his family closes ranks around him, shielding him from the world he stood atop of for so long.

Although I still talk to Nancy on a near-daily basis, I learned quickly not to ask about his condition. If she wanted to talk to me, fine, but it wasn't my place to bring it up. Since I started this book, though, I've been blessed—honored, really—to have Nancy uncharacteristically share some of the most personal details of her life as caregiver, opening up painful wounds that she has borne almost alone, moments she has shared with few people.

Nancy has also given me the green light to talk with others who have been sharing the load with her—her daughter, Patti, most notably—as well as a diverse network of friends with whom she talks regularly, an eclectic group that ranges from Casey Ribicoff to Warren Beatty and John McCain, connecting Hollywood and Washington and points in between.

If there has been one positive to come out of this long, painful experience, it has been the renewed closeness of the Reagan family. Media reports always exaggerated the rifts and ignored the bonds, but any family that includes two children by a previous marriage, a stepmother, and a sometimes blinding dose of limelight is going to have its problems. I think Nancy would be the first to say that over the years, particularly the White House years, her relationship with the kids was rocky. I have watched this give-and-take for nearly thirty-five years. The Reagans are like most of us; they have family problems. Who doesn't? But so much of that has disappeared over the last decade, largely because of the common concern for their father and husband, but also because of the illness and death of Reagan's oldest daughter, Maureen. Hard times such as the Reagans have been through seem to either splinter families or pull them together. Happily, it's been the latter for this group. I know that has been deeply gratifying for Nancy. Maybe it has been for the Gipper, too—more proof of his faith that everything happens for a reason.

The circle has even been extended to include Reagan's first wife, Jane Wyman. A short time after Reagan was diagnosed, Nancy placed a call to Jane, to let her know about the situation firsthand. Nancy offered to give her updates from time to time. When Jane and Ron's daughter—Maureen—lay dying, the two reached out again. At Maureen's service at the Sacramento Catholic Cathedral, they sat together, in the same pew as Maureen's husband, Dennis, and daughter, Rita.

What I have seen more than anything else in my phone chats with the former first lady and our regular lunches is a woman rising to the occasion time and time again.

Reagan quickly settled into a pattern in the early years of his disease. He would be driven to his Century City office late in the morning. Appointments would have been set up—most of them as innocuous and brief as young schoolchildren having their picture taken with him or newlyweds from Bel Air Presbyterian Church, to which the Reagans belonged, posing in their wedding finery for a photo with the former president.

After his brief "work" day, Reagan would have lunch in his office and then be driven home. Late in the day, he could often be seen taking a walk around a small public park in Bel Air, accompanied by a pair of Secret Service agents and his nurse. In the evenings, Nancy and Reagan still ate together in the dining room, but they were often quiet meals. There was no way to talk about the day, or share even the smallest experiences. Inevitably, Ronald Reagan's world got smaller week by week. Nancy's did, too, with her husband fading more and more.

Alzheimer's is unpredictable, unwieldy. Caregivers have to be creative day by day, but it has been found that people suffering from the disease are often comforted by repeated patterns of behavior and by tangible reminders of the life they used to live. In some Alzheimer's care facilities, a onetime librarian will be provided with books, an artist with paints and brushes and a canvas to work on. At one facility, the staff put up an eye chart in an unused closet, then hauled in a chair and a stool for a man who had been an optometrist.

I don't know if Nancy had read about this or if she was just doing what intuitively seemed to help Reagan. But she could see that the predictable routine they had fallen into seemed to ground him. She even made sure a schedule was printed up for him each day. He would keep it in his pocket and refer to it often. He had always had one as governor and president, and he had always been compulsively punctual, too. Now, with his schedule at hand and a watch on his wrist, he would arrive in his Century City office late in the morning for appointments that had been lined up for him to create a facsimile of the world he had once known.

It seems almost cynical, all this trickery, but it worked, at least for the time being. Nancy, though, has always been a realist. She knew that this phase wouldn't last, that she would have to accept whatever was waiting around the corner.

One of the things a public life, especially one in politics, teaches you is how to think ahead, especially how to come up with contingency plans. In my many years with the Reagans, I saw Nancy become very astute at doing just that. Oftentimes, the rest of us would be entirely caught up in the moment. Only the first lady would have really puzzled through the what-ifs and therefores of the crisis at hand. But this was different. With Alzheimer's, chains of causality get thrown out the window. You know the general direction: down, down, down. But you have no way of knowing how that will manifest itself. "You just take it one day at a time" became, in effect, Nancy's new mantra, and it was more than just words. She literally woke up each morning without a clue as to how that day was going to play out. "Put one foot in front of the other," she would remind herself, but that's so hard when you have so little idea what direction you're headed in and how long you are going to be allowed to go that way.

For a while, Nancy would still go to New York two or three times a year, just for a few days, to see friends, go out to dinner, maybe take in a play. The theater there always reminds Nancy of her mother, and her own early aspirations. More and more, though, her husband simply couldn't be left alone. She would have to find someone she trusted completely to stay with him—John Hutton filled that bill admirably when he was available—but even then, she couldn't escape an overwhelming sense of duty. Wherever she was visiting, Nancy would call home in the evenings. The phone had started to puzzle Reagan, but he was never confused by the sound of her voice coming through the receiver.

One of these trips to New York, in the fall of 1995, was to see her old pal and confidant Jerry Zipkin for a last time. (Another of Jerry's friends, Somerset Maugham, had used him as the model for Elliot Templeton in his 1944 novel **The Razor's Edge**.) Nancy and Patti, who was living in New York at the time, had visited with Jerry the day before, and it was clear that death was imminent. He passed away the following morning, and his funeral service was arranged for the next week. Under normal circumstances, Nancy would have stayed on to attend, but nothing was normal anymore. She felt that she couldn't stay away from home any longer than she had planned. Everyone at the service understood, and Jerry would have too, maybe most of all, but the choices get hard when a disease like Alzheimer's has muscled its way into your life.

Sometime in 1998, Reagan's days at the office became fewer and further between. His mornings started later, if they started at all. "Taking one day at a time" had been ratcheted up another notch.

Nancy tried to slow the decline. As her husband grew less able to interact with the outside world, Nancy tried to lead him on private tours through the many years they had shared. In the evenings, she would sit next to Reagan on the couch in the den and play some of the tapes from the White House or turn the pages of the dozens of scrapbooks that documented their public life—any attempt to keep his focus on the life they shared. Soon, she would be doing this alone.

She still tried to get him into the office for lunch, so he could sit where he had sat for years, looking out across the familiar view of the city while he ate, but the best-laid plans often fall apart with Alzheimer's patients. Reagan was sleeping more, which might have been a blessing for everyone.

She had no more luck with her efforts to take Reagan to his beloved ranch.

"I thought he'd still relate to that," Nancy told me. "I thought the ranch was a place that would always make him happy, no matter what."

Maybe it was too much space, too many vistas—the very things he once loved. I've never asked Nancy how she used to imagine these retirement years would be, but I'm sure Rancho del Cielo loomed large in her thoughts. It would have been a place, finally, just for the two of them, a chance to take long walks and enjoy the dazzling sunsets without some worried scheduler pushing them along to the next event, the next call, the next visitor. How expansive time would have seemed then! But Alzheimer's is a disease that tightens the world, narrows everything. Maureen Reagan had a poignant description of the disease: "You start out on a seven-hundred-acre ranch and end up in the living room."

The sale of the ranch was a powerful acknowledgment that Reagan's disease was running the show now.

By then, the Century City office sat empty, too. When even the lunches alone there became too much for him to handle, she said, **No more.** Protecting his dignity had moved to the top of her agenda, right along with guarding his privacy. Only the framed photographs on the shelves remained in Century City, a heartbreaking reminder of how things used to be.

Nancy was having her eyes examined at

UCLA's hospital in 2000 when an anxious Secret Service agent interrupted to say that the president had taken a spill while trying to get out of bed at the Reagans' Bel Air home. Nancy rushed back to find her husband in his bed, restless and rubbing his hip. Although he was well beyond telling his wife what had happened or where it hurt, she knew right away it was a broken hip. Nancy asked the Secret Service to find a private ambulance so he could be quietly shepherded to Saint John's Hospital. As she climbed in the ambulance to accompany her husband for the short ride, Nancy knew all too well what waited ahead. The absence of a shrieking siren could keep the media at bay only so long.

Over the years, I have fielded I don't know how many calls from the national media trying to confirm Ronald Reagan's demise, but at least for the president's retirement years, the broken hip and subsequent surgery to repair it took the cake. It got so bad that a CBS Los Angeles affiliate actually had the audacity to call Nancy at home to ask, and I quote, "if your husband has died." Nancy phoned me immediately afterward, and I was so furious I called my friend Bill Plante, a veteran of CBS's Washington bureau, to let him know that his network had gone beyond the pale. Within hours, Plante's boss in New York rang me up with an apology. I told him, "You're calling the wrong person." He graciously called Nancy, and the "death watch" seemed to slow down.

After Reagan was resting comfortably following surgery, I had a long chat with Nancy. As delicately as I could, I asked her if she thought this was "it." It didn't take a medical degree to figure out that Reagan was in the worst possible straits. A broken hip in a ninety-year-old man whose health was already compromised would seem to suggest that time was running out. Nancy knew all that, of course. She was a doctor's daughter. But she refused to give up.

"No," she assured me, "he's going to get well." Just to make sure, she had the hospital bring another bed into the room. She wasn't going anywhere.

Tragically, Reagan's first daughter, Maureen, was dying of cancer in the same hospital, at the same time. Maureen's melanoma had spread past treatment. Along with the other Reagan children and stepchildren—Michael, Patti, and Ron— Nancy shuttled between both rooms. She told her husband that his daughter was in another bed just yards away, but she wasn't sure he understood any of it.

"I'll never know," she said wistfully.

She'll never know, either, whether Reagan understood when she explained to him in August 2000 that Maureen had died, but Loyal Davis had once told Nancy that he never assumed a patient couldn't hear and understand him—even if the patient was under anesthesia or comatose. At the least, Nancy believed, she was telling Reagan's soul what had happened to his daughter. Even if his brain didn't register the words, his heart would understand.

Back home in Bel Air, Reagan began therapy to repair the injury and adjust to the new hip. I remember Nancy's telling me one day that the president was being very good about doing the rehab work. "He deals with it. Ronnie is very obliging; if you ask him to do something, he'll do it," she said.

But the fall and the broken hip had imposed yet another new reality on their lives. They would no longer be able to share a bed. There was no choice. He needed bars on either side, or he would repeat the same accident over and over again. Nancy ordered a hospital bed for him and set up a round-the-clock nursing station in the other room. After nearly half a century of sleeping beside her husband, she now had to sleep and wake up in a bed that felt empty and lonely.

It is a passage that's wrenching for anyone whose spouse is suffering from a long, incurable disease, a death before death. For the Reagans—both of them—I think the separation must have been as bad as it can get. Theirs was no ordinary love.

I had seen the intensity of the Reagans' relationship time and again, from that first glimpse when neither wanted to be the last to say good-bye to the way his eyes always lit up the minute Nancy entered a room. I had been privy, too, over the years to his diary entries. "Why is it whenever she is gone for ten minutes or more, I begin to worry," he once wrote. "And then, when she returns, everything is okay? Mommy is back." But even I, I have to admit, was blown away by the publication of **I Love You, Ronnie,** the collection of letters and poems that Reagan had written Nancy over the years. (Proceeds from the book benefit the Alzheimer's Association as well as the Ronald Reagan Presidential Foundation for the Reagan library and museum in Simi Valley, California.)

Occasionally in Washington, where I've lived for many years now, I'll hear sophisticates laugh at the book, but I have never heard that outside the Beltway, where people are less likely to look for sinister motives and are more open to pure expressions of the heart. Ronald Reagan might not have been a trained poet, but he was an old-fashioned romantic and not afraid to show it. One of the letters he wrote in 1963, can stand in a way for all of them:

If I ache, it's because we are apart and yet that can't be, because you are inside

and a part of me, so we really aren't apart at all.

Yet I ache, but wouldn't be without the ache, because that would mean being without you and that I can't be, because I love you.

Keats would have written it differently, but he could not have written more from the deep heart's core.

The milestones mount up for Nancy and Reagan—birthdays, anniversaries. They are bittersweet occasions without a lot of celebrating, but Nancy makes sure that her husband's room is decorated with balloons and that gifts are opened at his bedside. She still believes that, at some level, he understands. They celebrated their fiftieth wedding anniversary on March 4, 2003. Nancy said it was pretty lonely, in spite of a small cake and flowers.

"We had such an extraordinary life, but that somehow makes it harder," she told me. "There are so many memories that I can no longer share. I find myself starting to say, 'Do you remember . . . ' Then I have to stop myself."

Recently Nancy and I met for one of our regular lunches. I asked about Reagan's health. It's still a difficult topic, but Nancy knows that this is part of her role now. She is not only caregiver to the man who used to be president; she's also his only pipeline to the world. Often Nancy's response would be a brief, unvarnished description of his decline, but on this day she told me a story that had been passed on to her a year earlier by one of the agents on Reagan's Secret Service detail.

The year was probably 1999, and the president's memory was fading. Some days were better than others. On this particular one, Reagan was sitting quietly in his office off their bedroom when a Secret Service agent came in and asked if he would like to go for a walk.

As they walked alone down Beverly Boulevard in Beverly Hills, Reagan seemed quieter than usual. He seemed to be okay, the agent recounted, just hard to read. Before long, he stopped in front of a quaint blue house surrounded by a white picket fence. Beyond it, a rose garden graced the facade of the little bungalow. Reagan paused, then reached over the small gate, trying to lift the latch to gain entry. As he did so, the agent gently touched him on the hand with a warm admonishment. "We can't go in there, Mr. President; it isn't our house."

Reagan paused for a second before pulling his hand back from the latch. "I know," he said quietly, "but I just wanted to pick a rose for my love."

Nancy's eyes welled up as she told me the story. So did mine.

To this day, Nancy helps in the daily nursing and caring for her husband. One of the doctors told me that he watched as she eased Reagan back into bed after a brief walk one recent morning. She has learned to encourage him to sit on the edge of the bed. Then she gently lifts his feet and legs up as he settles back with his head on the pillow. When she had finished this time, Nancy looked at her Ronnie lying there alone, took off her shoes, and gently got into bed with him. She was putting her arms around him as the doctor quietly left the room.

All those stories over the years about her phony "stare," all that snickering about how the two of them always held hands like a couple of ninth graders on a date—they just don't mean much anymore. In the face of this one, true thing, everything else falls away.

ACKNOWLEDGMENTS

There are many people I need to thank for helping me with this project. The first of course is Nancy Reagan. It's not easy to write about one of your best friends, but her openness, candor, and support made this book possible. I am indebted to her in too many ways to count.

I also want to thank those who shared their many memories of Nancy, especially Patti Davis, Mike Wallace, Warren Beatty, Joe Califano, Sheila Tate, Fred Ryan, Joanne Drake, Stu Spencer, Dr. John Hutton, Casey Ribicoff, Lou Cannon, Bob Strauss, Doug Wick, Dennis Revell, and Dr. Richard Davis.

I thank my friends who helped me behind the scenes, especially Bill Adler, Diana Walker, Mauro DiPreta, Howard Means, and Jeff Surrell.

PHOTOGRAPH CAPTIONS

1. Family photo—Ron, Ron Jr., Nancy, and Patti in Pacific Palisades, California, 1960.

2. It seemed like Nancy and Ron were always arm-in-arm. They hated to be apart. The joy they exuded when they were together spread to others, including me.

3. A weaker President Reagan leaving George Washington University Hospital on April, 11, 1981, a few days after the assassination attempt. With the couple is their daughter, Patti Davis.

4. By the end of the year, Reagan was back to his usual self—and so was Nancy. Here they are enjoying themselves in the White House. Nancy always brightened the man up, and this day, November 9, 1981, was no exception.

5. Nancy was always the gracious hostess—she was known for that, of course. Here she introduces me to Mrs. Mubarak, the wife of the president of Egypt, at a state dinner on February 3, 1982.

6. The crowd at the Gridiron Club appreciated Nancy's self-mocking parody. It received national attention in every paper. Bolstered by the warmer coverage, Nancy felt more comfortable elevating her profile to do good works.

7. Here's the three of us watching the midterm election returns in 1982. We had a good feeling about it by this point.

8. One of Ron and Nancy's favorite pastimes: horseback riding at their ranch in California.

9. Nancy was known as being prim and proper, but she always loved to have fun. Here she surprised the love of her life with a birthday cake—in the middle of a press briefing! February 4, 1983.

10. Christmas 1983: Here me and my wife, Caroline, flank the president and first lady, in front of the ever-glorious White House

Christmas tree, in which Nancy took such pride. She always loved the holidays.

11. I was surprised when Nancy took up drug abuse as a cause. She told me, "I was stunned to find out just how large the problem of drug abuse really is," and she really ran with it. It touched her in a truly personal way.

12. Nancy went through many difficult times at the White House. Through her struggle with cancer she always held her head high, and coped with it as well as one can while in the public eye. Nancy didn't have the luxury of privacy, so she did the next best thing: used her diagnosis and subsequent mastectomy as a kind of national teachable moment.

13. In March 2001, Nancy christened the aircraft carrier USS Ronald Reagan, with President George W. Bush and shipbuilding CEO William Frick looking on. The president would say of Nancy: "At every step of an amazing life, Nancy Reagan has been at Ronald Reagan's side. Right by his side. As his optimism inspired us, her love and devotion strengthened him." (White House photograph by Eric Draper)